S0-CWP-618

Dedicated to
Charles Covert Arensberg,
co-founder and chairman of the
Pittsburgh History & Landmarks Foundation,
who has inspired our organization for 25 years.

Some things are saved: here, the "Ladies of Stone" survive the 1966 demolition of the Fourth Avenue Post Office.

A PAST STILL ALIVE

THE PITTSBURGH HISTORY & LANDMARKS FOUNDATION CELEBRATES
TWENTY-FIVE YEARS

Walter C. Kidney

1989

Published by the
Pittsburgh History & Landmarks Foundation
450 The Landmarks Building, One Station Square
Pittsburgh, PA 15219-1170
Copyright © 1989, Pittsburgh History & Landmarks Foundation
Manufactured in the United States of America

Author
Walter C. Kidney

Project Director, Editor
Louise King Ferguson

Library of Congress Catalog Card Number: 89-62940
ISBN 0-916670-13-9

Illustration Sources

All illustrations not noted are from the Pittsburgh History & Landmarks Foundation files.

Public Relations Department, Aluminum Company of America: 19 (bottom, left)

Art Work of Pittsburgh (1893; P.H.L.F. collection): 1, 11 (top), 26 (top, right, and bottom), 36 (bottom), 41 (top), 42

Art Work of Pittsburgh (1899; P.H.L.F. collection): 23 (top), 31 (top)

Pittsburgh Photographic Library, Carnegie Library of Pittsburgh: 3, 4 (bottom), 5, 7 (bottom), 8 (top), 9, 11 (bottom, left), 15 (middle), 16 (top), 17 (bottom), 18 (top), 19 (top and bottom, right), 22, 23 (bottom), 25 (bottom), 26 (top, left), 27 (right), 29, 30 (top and bottom, right), 31 (bottom), 32 (top, left), 33 (left), 37 (top and bottom, right), 38, 44, 45 (top and bottom, left), 46, 55 (top), 64 (bottom), 80, 82 (bottom), 91 (top), 92 (bottom), 102 (bottom), 103 (top), 104, 106 (top), 107 (bottom), 109

Deeter, Ritchey & Sippel: 62 (bottom)

Golomb Photographers, Inc.: 71 (bottom), 116 (top), 131 (left column, top)

Clyde Hare: 13 (bottom), 24 (top), 47 (bottom), 55 (bottom, left and right), 66 (top), 67, 70, 77, 78, 79, 81 (top), 94 (bottom), 96, 97, 99 (bottom), 105, 110, 111, 112, 114, 115 (top), 132 (left column, top and middle, center column, bottom), 133 (center column, top), 134 (left column, top, center column, top)

Landmarks Design Associates: 68

Arthur Lubetz Associates: 85 (bottom)

Randy Nelson, Invision: 116 (bottom), 117 (bottom), 130 (right column, top and bottom), 132 (right column)

Notas Interesantes Acerca de Pittsburgh (1888; P.H.L.F. collection): 34

Pennsylvania Historic Resource Survey: 35 (bottom)

L.P. Perfido Associates: 85 (top)

Pittsburgh & Lake Erie Railroad: 63 (bottom)

Pittsburgh City Photographer Collection, Archives of Industrial Society, University of Pittsburgh: 6, 33 (bottom, right), 90, 100 (bottom)

Martha Rial: 134 (left column, bottom)

Mary Roberts Rinehart et al, *Words Warm and Significant* (Boggs & Buhl, 1924; P.H.L.F. collection): 15 (top)

Congregation Rodef Shalom: 32 (bottom, left)

St. Paul's Monastery: 86 (top, right)

Society for the Preservation of the Duquesne Heights Incline: 73

This Is an Urban Area (Oakland Corporation, c. 1963; P.H.L.F. collection): 47 (top), 76

Maurice Tierney: 69 (top)

Maureen Wikiera: 61 (top), 135 (center column, top)

Trustees

Charles Covert Arensberg
Clifford A. Barton
Mrs. Jeanne B. Berdik
Mark Stephen Bibro
Mrs. Kenneth S. Boesel
Charles H. Booth, Jr.
Mrs. Susan Brandt
J. Judson Brooks
Anthony J. Bryan
Donald C. Burnham
Mrs. Guy Burrell
Paul Cain
C. Dana Chalfant, Sr.
Mrs. James H. Childs, Jr.
Frederic L. Cook
John P. Davis, Jr.
Hon. Michael M. Dawida
Mrs. Robert Dickey III
George C. Dorman
Arthur J. Edmunds
Richard D. Edwards
Mrs. Leonore R. Elkus
Alan S. Fellheimer
James R. Ferry
Hon. D. Michael Fisher
Mrs. James A. Fisher
Floyd R. Ganassi
Mrs. David L. Genter
Richard E. Givens
Hon. Barbara Hafer
Mrs. Ethel Hagler
Dr. Leon L. Haley
Charles E. Half
Sen. H. John Heinz III
Mrs. Henry P. Hoffstot, Jr.
Henry P. Hoffstot, Jr.
Dr. Frances Holland
Thomas O. Hornstein
Carl Hughes
Torrence M. Hunt, Sr.
Paul R. Jenkins
James W. Knox
G. Christian Lantzsch

Mrs. Alan G. Lehman
Chester LeMaistre
Aaron P. Levinson
Edward J. Lewis
Hon. Frank J. Lucchino
Eugene A. March
Grant McCargo
DeCourcy E. McIntosh
Theodore Merrick
Philip F. Muck
Hon. Thomas Murphy
William R. Oliver
Robert F. Patton
Mrs. Evelyn B. Pearson
Mrs. Nathan W. Pearson
Hon. Mark H. Pollock
Mrs. S. Raymond Rackoff
Don Riggs
Dan Rooney
Mrs. Sidney Ruffin
Richard M. Scaife
Mrs. Steven J. Smith
G. Whitney Snyder
William P. Snyder III
Furman South III
Miles Span
M. B. Squires, Jr.
Merrill Stabile
William Strickland
Dr. Imilda Tuttle
Dr. Albert C. Van Dusen
Hon. Douglas Walgren
Mrs. James M. Walton
Mrs. Robert Wardrop
James L. Winokur
Mrs. Alan E. Wohleber
George H. Yeckel
Wilbert Young
Arthur P. Ziegler, Jr.

Emeritus
Edward C. Quick
James D. Van Trump

Acknowledgements

The publication of *A Past Still Alive* was made possible in part by the Pittsburgh History & Landmarks Foundation Revolving Fund for Education, which was established in 1984 through a generous grant from the Claude Worthington Benedum Foundation. Revenues from Station Square, a mixed-use development of the Pittsburgh History & Landmarks Foundation, have partly underwritten the cost of this publication.

Contents

Foreword

Twenty-five years is barely one tenth of Pittsburgh's history as a city or Allegheny County's existence as a home for the European American. But it is a relatively long time for the preservation movement. We can find some pride in this length of time for our Foundation, as we were one of the earliest county-wide organized movements in the United States. In that time also, we feel, we have made some visible marks on the city and county, marks which we believe enhance the pride we Pittsburghers feel for our place in the sun. Walter Kidney well describes these marks on our landscape in these essays.

Pittsburgh is a better place to live in than it was in 1964. True, there have been vast upheavals in that time in our industry. The smoke and flames of the "Workshop of the World" have gone with the wind. But there is a new Pittsburgh now, ready to remember its past and honor its builders, but dedicated to finding new means of livelihood, new industry in the cleaner air along the cleaner rivers of our wonderful Western Pennsylvania hills and valleys. We look forward to the twenty-first century: new architecture to encourage, new ways to preserve the indissoluble link to our past. As Shakespeare says in *Timon of Athens* (Act II, Scene 2): "The future comes apace: What shall defend the interim?"

Charles Covert Arensberg
Chairman

What We Have Lost

A city of any age at all casts off its older structures as a locust does its skin, growing, finding its older shell too confining, creating a new one. Most of its buildings are inherently mortal, built to last only as long as they serve their purposes. The door in which a shiny key was turned with pride a century ago lies flat on the ground beside a heap of battered rubble. The much-needed bridge at last comes down, making way for a much-needed bridge. The proud facade, caught between its original vogue and a revived one, yields to a building in the enlightened taste of the moment. Even a hill is shaved down, and a ravine filled in. A city of any age is a palimpsest, old markings scraped off and new ones added with a flourish: and the scraping knife always handy.

Thousands of structures in the Pittsburgh region have gone over two centuries of history, and with each an expenditure of skill and brute force. Some went because of circumstances that seemed compelling, some because they had no apparent further use, or were out of fashion, or because of fire or other accident. The structures illustrated in this essay came down because of someone's decision, not because of accident, and most came down in the 1950s and '60s. If some yielded to compelling circumstances, others might have been saved by a little imagination, a sympathetic buyer, or an organized preservation effort. But this was not yet the time for such things, and the time came slowly. James D. Van Trump's articles in *Charette* and elsewhere, beginning in 1956, at least revealed some of the almost-unknown architectural history of the region and called attention to places taken for granted. Preservation in Pittsburgh can hardly be said to have existed, though, until 1964, when the Pittsburgh History & Landmarks Foundation was organized. A handful of conspicuous places like the Blockhouse, the Jail, and the Courthouse

Above: The Arbuthnot and Harper buildings, under construction on Liberty Avenue in 1892. Replaced by a wing of Benedum Center. Opposite: The Manchester Bridge comes down, 1970.

Victorian decorative work in Manchester.

had been saved in the past by public protest or, as in the case of the first, by purchase, but the saving of an entire neighborhood or of a building of less than celebrity status had probably never been contemplated. In these Renaissance decades the emphasis was on the glitteringly new and the demonstrably utilitarian, on prestige and profit, not on the grimy past that was something of a badge of shame.

Someone had, then, to reveal the potential of the architecture under the soot and flaking paint, appeal to eyes starved of ornament and picturesqueness by Modern architecture, make vivid to the citizen places that had become too familiar; show that repairs and adaptations could be made to buildings, one by one, rather than losing them to comprehensive redevelopment. When founded in 1964, one of Landmarks' first tasks was to help organize neighborhood groups to demand more than quantitative official standards for housing, buy and rehabilitate properties to set the example and, more and more, educate the public in what it had, and could lose. In consequence of Landmarks' activities, and of a general public opposition to massive demolitions—the populist uprising against the East Street Valley condemnation practices in the late 1960s, for instance—the preservationist influence is now much more of a power. The demolitions of valuable places have not wholly ceased, but preservation has created an inertia to oppose massive, disorienting change at high speed.

The structures shown here were for the most part notable in their day, and constitute by no means the greater part of those lost. We may spare a sigh or two as well for such lesser victims, quite numerous, as the ordinary East End house, its porch gone, its wounds patched up after a fashion, and its brickwork painted. On these too is the mark of the rootless 1950s and '60s.

The losses we have suffered are due to causes whose real explanation may be impossible to determine. Take the removal of the bronze cheneaux, the ornamental cornice trim, on the Carnegie Institute. When a new aluminum roof went onto the building in 1957 they were removed, and with the removal the building lost some of its panache. The reason given was the danger of electrolysis between the two metals; but might not the cheneaux have been recast in aluminum with a suitable finish? The real reason was perhaps that such highly-

Above: the vanished skyline of Ridge Avenue. Right: Forbes Avenue front of the Carnegie Institute with its crowning cheneau, 1907–57. Alden & Harlow, architects.

decorated features were out of fashion, and that the old was to make a gesture toward the new, like a modern nun with her raised hemline.

Fashion may account for much that was done around this time. The Press Building, a very pleasant essay in 1920s Italian Romanesque, was clad in sheet metal around this same time, presumably as another gesture of modernity; an army of restorers with can openers may some day reveal to us, once again, one of downtown Pittsburgh's nicer buildings. The Farmers Deposit National Bank of Alden & Harlow, in the 500 block of Wood Street, was not the definitive artistic solution to the skyscraper problem; it followed the old solution of pelting the great bulk with architectural motifs until it was subdued. But the gray-brown sheet-metal cladding it has had for two decades has given it a specious modernity totally without character. These are drastic alterations of old buildings, but outright destruction may also be due to fashion rather than necessity.

On the other hand, the demolition in 1907 of the Union Bridge of 1874 seems to have been appropriate. A wooden covered bridge built in the Iron City—actually, one of three built around the same time—was an oddity in the first place; and especially after 1885, when the Davis Island Dam maintained a high pool level, such a low bridge was a navigational frustration.

Roebling's St. Clair or Sixth Street Bridge yielded much earlier to a Theodore Cooper bridge capable of bearing the load of electric streetcars, and this was understandable enough. That the McArdle Roadway bridge, tailored in a gentle Modernistic by Stanley Roush, had to come down was due, the City claimed,

Above: original facing, 1903–c. 1967, of the Farmers Deposit National Bank Building, downtown. Alden & Harlow, architects. Right: second Sixth Street Bridge, 1859–92. John Augustus Roebling, engineer. Opposite, above: Union Bridge, 1874–1907. Opposite, below: third Sixth Street Bridge, 1892–1926; now re-erected between Neville Island and Coraopolis. Theodore Cooper, engineer.

to its deteriorated concrete work; but whether this was worse off than that of the Westinghouse Bridge, which *has* been repaired, is to be doubted. It may for one reason or another have been inexpedient to keep the Roush bridge, conspicuous though it was against the side of Mount Washington, but it probably was too remote from current fashion to call for extra cash or concern.

Planning imperatives took other places, though one might wonder in a few cases if the grand scheme may have been too strong in the planners' minds. On the Point State Park site the Exposition Buildings and the Manchester Bridge had certainly had an uneasy relationship for years, with a wooden traffic ramp crossing in front of the buildings to reach the high level mandated by the Army Engineers—at last—for steamboat clearance. This was hardly harmonious visually, the ramp itself had grown perilous, and the buildings had

Below: Mount Washington (P. J. McArdle) Roadway Bridge, 1927–c. 1983. Stanley L. Roush, architect. Opposite, above: Manchester Bridge, Allegheny River at the Point, 1915–70. Bureau of Works, City of Pittsburgh, engineers; Charles Keck, sculptor. Opposite, below: Exposition Buildings, near the Point, 1901-51. D. H. Burnham & Co., architects.

long been unused in the early 1950s when they came down. Might one or the other have been kept and integrated into the park? It may not have occurred to the planners to consider the matter, and the foreseeable future may not have allowed a Yes in any case.

In the adjoining Gateway Center area, was there any point in saving the pompous Wabash Terminal, its rear uncovered since the 1946 burning of its trainshed? Could the old-fashioned floor plan have accommodated new offices? The contemporary Pittsburgh & Lake Erie Railroad Station, its office space at present well-tenanted, suggests possibilities but in any case the Terminal yielded to Gateway Four. What about the Shoenberger house on lower Penn Avenue in the Gateway Center area? Toward the last a veterans' organization had covered its Italianate front with fake fieldstone and perhaps its detail had been knocked off in the process, and it is true that a city house looks odd detached from others of its kind; but had anyone even thought of some way of keeping it, or was it only so much brick to crumble as the headache ball swung?

On the Lower Hill, everything but a church was eliminated in the late 1950s to make way for a projected, showy acropolis of apartment houses and cultural institutions. Perhaps the blight there was hopeless, but a neighborhood was destroyed and its people dispersed

Above: John Shoenberger house, downtown, c. 1847–1950. John Chislett(?), architect.

Pittsburgh, Pa., Interior Wabash Depot.

Right: The waiting room of the Wabash Terminal, downtown, 1904–55. Theodore C. Link, architect. Opposite: exterior.

Above: Lower Hill, c. 1955. Below, left: Lower Hill, mid-1960s. Below, right: YWCA on Chatham Street, Lower Hill. Janssen & Abbott, architects.

for a grand plan that in important ways was never realized, and the chance for a rehabilitated residential neighborhood next to the Triangle was lost.

As to other plans: Frank Furness' Baltimore & Ohio Station just east of the town end of the Smithfield Street Bridge was undoubtedly out of fashion, and the shore-hugging Parkway was planned to come right where it stood. In a time of declining rail passenger service, there was perhaps no case to present. Another highway project, that of I-279, ate the heart out of Dutchtown on the North Side around 1970, destroying churches, stores, and houses that had been placed close to a local crossroads that has now become regional and more than regional as a traffic node. Perhaps it was unavoidable that they should go, but the sovereign presence of so much concrete, so many restless cuts and ramps, is like seared tissue that will never heal.

Top: Baltimore and Ohio Railroad Station, downtown, 1887–c. 1955. Frank Furness, architect. Above and left: First St. John's Evangelical Lutheran Church, Dutchtown, 1870–1971. James Balph, architect.

11

*I-279 clearances. Right: East Street houses near St.
Boniface Church. Below: East Street Valley in 1974.
Opposite, above: East Ohio Street buildings in the demolition area. Opposite, below: I-279 in Dutchtown, nearing
completion.*

Above: houses on the West Commons, North Side. Below; original Allegheny Town area before the clearings of 1961.

Unlike Manchester and the Mexican War Streets, the original Allegheny Town, enclosed by the Commons and a third of a mile square, was submitted to conventional urban renewal from 1961 on. The planners believed, it seemed, that nothing could be done with what was there. The North Side had been in a decline for years, and even Boggs and Buhl's, a department store once famous, had gone out of business. The ideas of organizing the inhabitants, showing the latent architectural quality and rehabilitation potential of what was there, turning attention to the buildings one by one, were not yet developed. Public buildings, usually in good condition, survived in the area to some extent, though the Allegheny Market House of 1863 was replaced by grass and an apartment slab; Ober Park was transmogrified into a concrete pit; and Andrew Carnegie's memorial of gratitude to Colonel James Anderson, who had started his education, was dissected.

Right: Boggs and Buhl's, demolished c. 1961. Below: Federal Street and Stockton Avenue, c. 1960. Bottom, left: original Allegheny Town area, c. 1970. Bottom, right: element of the Anderson Memorial, after dispersal.

Top: Fort Wayne Station, North Side, 1906–c. 1965. Price & McLanahan, architects. Left: cast-iron shopfront in the cleared area. Above: Allegheny Center Mall.

Allegheny Market House, Ohio and Federal Streets, 1863-1966. Architect unknown.

Urban renewal in East Liberty took one of Carnegie's libraries, a gravely handsome structure. Much earlier, St. Pierre Ravine was filled in to make Schenley Plaza, and in the process the Bellefield Bridge, less than two decades old, was buried and used as the foundation of the Schenley Fountain. At the abortive Oakland hillside campus for the University of Pittsburgh, State Hall, one of the very few executed portions of Henry Hornbostel's spectacular master plan, came down to yield ground for the present Chemistry Building, which

Top: Carnegie Library, East Liberty, c. 1900–c. 1960. Alden & Harlow, architects. Above: Bellefield Bridge, Schenley Park, built 1898, buried c. 1915. Henry B. Rust, engineer. Right: State Hall, University of Pittsburgh, c. 1910–c. 1970. Henry Hornbostel, architect.

flourishes ductwork much as the older building did terra-cotta decoration.

Development on less than an urbanistic scale and a lack of interest in keeping an older building under modern conditions caused a grimmer harvest. Kaufmann's found it expedient to remove its Modernistic interior by Janssen & Cocken in the 1960s; away went the black-and-white Carrara glass, and the Boardman Robinson *History of Commerce* murals on canvas eventually passed into Landmarks' hands. The Nixon,

Left: Interior, Kaufmann's department store, downtown, 1930–c. 1965. Janssen & Cocken, architects; Boardman Robinson, muralist. Below, left and right: Nixon Theatre, downtown, 1902–50. T. H. Marshall, architect.

once called the perfect theater, simply gave way to the Alcoa Building. The Jenkins Arcade, the last commercial arcade in the city, was demolished for Fifth Avenue Place, its many small offices and shops replaced by open office space along with the gesture of a small arcade. For Benedum Center and CNG Tower, two Romanesque commercial buildings on Liberty Avenue and the Moose Building on Penn Avenue disappeared. The Moose Building, because of its historic role as, in some sense, the Independence Hall of Czechoslovakia and because of its grandiose Beaux-Arts design, was especially missed, but was needed for a truck access. Landmarks, unable to save it, at least salvaged some of its terra cotta; further, Landmarks obtained a governmental agreement to no further demolition between Benedum Center and the Convention Center, thus preserving several blocks of turn-of-the-century commercial buildings, submittal of a National Register nomination, and grants for facade restoration. In Oakland the Carrier-Schmertz house and the adjacent Gardens, the car barn turned into a sports arena, were replaced by a big and very plain apartment house.

Below: Moose Building, downtown, 1915–84. Ulysses J. L. Peoples, architect. Below, right, and opposite: Jenkins Arcade, downtown, 1911-83. O. M. Topp, architect.

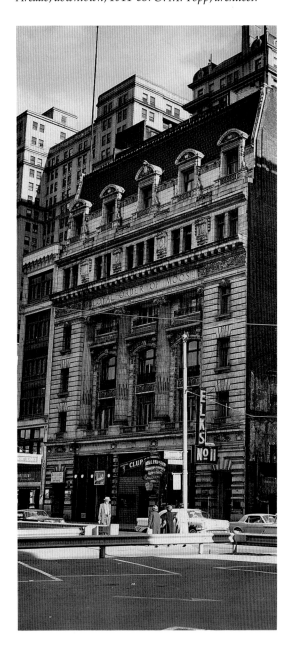

Above: Carrier-Schmertz house, Oakland, c. 1870–c. 1955. Isaac Hobbs & Sons, architects. Right: Duquesne Gardens (the Gardens), c. 1890–1956. Designer unknown. Opposite: Allegheny Arsenal, Lawrenceville, 1814 and after–1907 and after.

In some of these situations the power of insensitive planners was probably to be felt. In others, a lack of means or interest to keep the place up was more likely the cause: a vacuum into which something or at times nothing entered. The old Allegheny Arsenal had long been a dead letter when the Army gave it up in 1907, and bit by bit its buildings were stripped away until now very little is left. Between Butler Street and the Allegheny River is haphazard industry now, and up the hillside lie a grandiose and admittedly handsome school, a pleasant park, and some County buildings, the last three features at least agreeable substitutes for the savor of early history.

Above: Mount St. Peter, New Kensington, built 1940–44. Msgr. Nicola Fusco, designer. Below: R. B. Mellon house, Squirrel Hill, 1909–40. Alden & Harlow, architects.

Mansions of course, despite their bold here-to-stay and who-are-you? look, are terribly vulnerable over the decades. They place large demands on those who would live in them with adequate service and tight roofs, and if people without mansion mentalities and mansion funds are lacking, they tend to disappear. The economic expediencies they flouted have the ultimate revenge. Here is an assortment of these places now gone, replaced by other buildings or by bare earth. The Richard Beatty Mellon house starts us off as easily as may be, for its grounds are now Mellon Park and its fabric was cannibalized in the 1940s for the construction and adornment of Mount St. Peter in New Kensington; up there, the dry bones rose again with considerable success. The nearby "Lyndhurst," which long brooded over the corner of Fifth and Beechwood, seems to have disappeared without a trace. The same fate overcame the Rowe house, a mild surprise once on Morewood Avenue that is now replaced by three commonplace houses; the A. E. W. Painter house on Brighton

Above: "Lyndhurst," shown with added loggia, c. 1887 and after–1942 or later. Theophilus Parsons Chandler(?), architect. Left: Wallace H. Rowe house, Shadyside, 1902–c. 1961. Rutan & Russell, architects.

Above: Shoenberger villa, Lawrenceville, c. 1837–1949. John Chislett(?), architect. Right: A. E. W. Painter house, Allegheny West, 1887–c. 1960. Longfellow, Alden & Harlow, architects. Below: Ridge Avenue, North Side, in 1892.

Road, replaced by nothing; and the Shoenberger villa in Allegheny Cemetery, decrepit toward the last and replaced by graves. On Ridge Avenue in Allegheny a whole block front of mansions and near-mansions, once the pride of that city, ended a slightly rackety existence in the late 1960s when the Community College of Allegheny County wanted to build; there, Landmarks salvaged decorative work at least from the Denny and Oliver houses before the row was swept away. More salvage was carried out at "Picnic House" in Stanton Heights. The villa that a fond father built to entice his daughter and her unwelcome husband from England back to Pittsburgh failed of its purpose but hung on a century more. Two of its fancy interiors eventually were drawn into the eclectic interior of the Cathedral of Learning. "Fairacres," representative of the great country-house period in Sewickley Heights, did not quite make it to its fiftieth birthday. The home of the plant superintendent at the U.S. Steel Homestead Works, actually in Munhall, was not so much a mansion as top-level employee housing, yet it had the air of a *manoir* if not a *château*, the home of one under the power of others but who had himself power over many more; it went over a quarter-century ago, and there is only bare land in its place. Francis Lovejoy's house, never finished, came down in 1929 though his Annex, garage, stable, and gymnasium, survived long as a studio building, a well-known feature of the Park Place district. Many other great houses have had a hard fall in Pittsburgh, beginning in the 1930s.

Left: exterior of "Picnic House," Lawrenceville, c. 1835–1950. Above: ballroom as photographed in the early 1930s.

*"Grandview," the Phipps-Braun house, Squirrel Hill,
1901–79. J. Edward Keirn, architect. Above: entrance
front. Right: main hall. Opposite: "Fairacres," Sewickley
Heights, 1919–64. Hiss & Weekes, architects.*

Public and institutional buildings share this awkwardness as regards continuing use. City Hall ceased to function as such in 1917, and served humbler functions; once the city's pride but later hopelessly out of fashion, it disappeared without much regret. The Fourth Avenue Post Office, much remodeled over the years, survived into the early Landmarks period, allowing at least the salvage of the pediment statues and some of the sumptuous interior woodwork. St. Margaret's Hospital in Lawrenceville, regarded as an architectural scheme, smothered itself to death. Ernest Flagg's Classical ensemble, quite advanced in such a Romanesque town, was gradually obscured by expansions until, in the late 1970s, the Hospital moved out and built anew. The Duquesne Carnegie Library had been one of the library-club-concert halls that Andrew Carnegie built outside his own steel plants; the endowment ran out, the Library was given to the Board of Education, and

Above: City Hall, downtown, 1872–1952. Joseph W. Kerr, architect. Below, right: Fourth Avenue Post Office, downtown, 1891–1966. William Freret and James T. Windrim, architects. Below, left: salvaged pediment sculpture by Eugenio Pedon against the Post Office ruins.

Left: St. Margaret's Hospital, Lawrenceville, 1891–1961 and after. Ernest Flagg, architect. Below: Carnegie Free Library, Duquesne, c. 1900–1968. Alden & Harlow, architects.

disappeared. The convent of Our Lady of Charity, whose gables and towers were such a feature of the Troy Hill skyline, may not have been much occupied toward the last, and have not seemed worth the upkeep. The same may have been true of the Rodef Shalom temple on Eighth Street downtown, later the Second United Presbyterian Church, which vanished quietly from its side-street lot; and of the Third United Presbyterian Church, much more conspicuously placed at Shady and Northumberland in Squirrel Hill.

More utilitarian structures exist, frankly, on a produce-or-perish basis. Since the Carnegie and Bessemer Buildings were replaced, respectively, by an annex to Kaufmann's and a parking garage, it may be that their plans were unadaptable to modern requirements—though the Bessemer's near-twin, the Fulton Building, does survive. Shadyside Station lived on after commuter service ended, was a clubhouse for a while, then disappeared. The Penn Incline from the Hill to the Strip,

Above: Our Lady of Charity convent, Troy Hill, c. 1880–c. 1960. Architect unknown. Below: Congregation Rodef Shalom (Second United Presbyterian Church), downtown, c. 1901–c. 1960. Charles Bickel, architect. Right: Third United Presbyterian Church, Squirrel Hill, 1907–62. T. C. Chandler, architect.

*Left: Carnegie Building, downtown, 1895–1952. Long-
fellow, Alden & Harlow, architects. Top: Bessemer Building, downtown, 1906 c. 1964. Grosvenor Atterbury,
architect. Above: Shadyside Station, Pennsylvania Railroad, 1887–c. 1960. Wilson Brothers, architects.*

a mighty affair handling 20-ton loads, came down because it was losing money hopelessly. The same reasoning saw to the end of the Eliza Furnaces at Jones & Laughlin and of Dorothy Six at Duquesne.

You can look at pictures of these bygone places, in many instances recall them from your own memories. Of the ones that disappeared further back in time you may be a little incredulous: Did that *really* stand at that street corner? Did people really accept *that* as a normal and permanent feature of their world? A wooden covered bridge? A pompous federal building, not a parking garage? A mansion, not bland little houses? So strong: massive, but in the course of time gossamer. We too of course: not massive perhaps, but not permanent.

How much of the loss was necessary? How much do we wish we still had? The first question, a futile one now except for any educational value, would have to be considered case by case. As to the second, we would

Penn (18th Street) Incline, Hill to Strip, 1883–1953. Samuel Diescher, engineer.

*Above: Eliza Furnaces, Pittsburgh
Works, Jones & Laughlin Steel Cor-
poration, c. 1910–1983. Left: Dorothy
Six Furnace, Duquesne Works,
United States Steel Corporation,
1961–88.*

Above: Market Square c. 1920, looking north. Below: same view in 1892.

probably like to have almost everything if the sacrifice were not too great, if the continued presence of the place still had some meaning in the present-day environment. Suppose "Picnic House," the Arsenal buildings, the Fourth Avenue Post Office, the Duquesne Library existed, well-kept and active, their sordid, idle years behind them. Chaste and simple brick, florid carved stone, level rooflines, Romantic rooflines, intimate interiors, dramatic courtyards: products of ingenuity and labor still repaying the investments of long ago. From the aesthete's viewpoint little of quality replaced what we have seen here, and we can conclude that we are that much the poorer.

Above: 1100 block of Penn Avenue with the Allegheny River behind, 1916. Left: view westward on Sixth Avenue, c. 1910. Below: corner of Grant and Diamond Streets looking north. St. Peter's Episcopal Church (foreground) is now replaced by the Frick Building and St. Paul's Cathedral beyond by the Union Trust Building. Diamond Street is now Forbes Avenue.

What Remains, and Why

We might well have lost the places cited here, seen them obliterated or marred. That they remain was due on a few occasions to chance, but much more often to public protest or positive ideas for re-use. In some instances the places were threatened by development plans; in others, they were in a state of decay, underuse, or abandonment, and their removal would have been a matter of time. We say "places" because even geographical features have been under threat from time to time, not structures alone.

In many cases the threat has been from a narrow-visioned attitude that, for want of a better word, can be called utilitarian. This attitude can understand commercial growth, traffic movement, housing standards, etc., and knows the latest standard formulas and procedures related to these matters. It can also understand the latest planning fashions. But there its understanding stops. It is not against beauty and culture, if only because some people seem to want them, but it sees them as something to be institutionalized, confined to specific places. Thus, it admits to its urban vision a neatly-arranged park or plaza, an art museum, a symphony, a public library system, public sculpture chosen by consultants, and the like. It admits corporate art programs, and has nothing against art as a domestic pleasure. These things somehow enhance the image of a city. But that beauty and a sense of permanence in the midst of change should be on the ordinary street, present when one walks out the front door, is beyond its conception. An old neighborhood is judged as "housing stock," and *ipso facto* a reproach to a modern city in its oldness. The rehabilitation of the old houses one by one seems pointless when nice, neat new housing can be built in quantity to the latest standards. A conspicuous modernity, a neatness of effect, a demonstrable effi-

Above: Old housing stock, Central North Side. Opposite: Diamond Street, which is now Forbes Avenue, in the early 1950s. Gateway Center rises in the background.

The progressive image of the Pittsburgh Renaissance called for Modern architecture, which seemed to look something like this.

ciency in attaining the specific purpose for which a building or a highway is designed are the content of the utilitarian aesthetic. Certain places, just a few, may survive or be brought back in replica as being "historic" and be institutionalized like the art, but history need not be found in the streets. And idiosyncratic structures, violators of planners' rules, are thoroughly unwelcome. Design is by the book rather than by personality and need and individual situation.

Such an attitude was strongest in the 1950s and '60s. Economic survival became economic triumph, and the new Pittsburgh tended rather to reject the old. The city's past in many areas was visibly Victorian, and the vogue for that period's numerous architectural styles had not quite returned. The very dirt on the Victorian walls was a legacy of the Smoky City now so happily left in the past. Steel could hardly be ignored, with Jones & Laughlin's new open-hearth plant emitting smoke, however light, from eleven great stacks; but it could be downplayed, and one councilman in the 1960s had a scheme for camouflaging the Eliza Furnaces that made such a dramatic feature of the Parkway's turn to run along the Monongahela River.

It is surprising to consider the places in the Pittsburgh region that have been in danger, and the specific threats against them can be surprising too.

Bouquet's Redoubt, the "Blockhouse," was in danger a century ago from a Pennsylvania Railroad freight terminal that was getting bigger and bigger. The Redoubt was an authentic part of the Fort Pitt of the 1760s, the only part to remain barring some fragments of brickwork, and the only 18th-century building left in the Triangle. These considerations outweighed for history-lovers the fact that, being built in 1764, it had missed both the French and Indian War and the Pontiac Uprising. In the early 19th century it was serving, with makeshift additions, as a house, and while occasional journalists and photographers remembered it as a memento of early times nothing was done to preserve and restore it. In 1893, though, Mary Schenley, our famous expatriate, bought the property and gave it to the Daughters of the American Revolution. They restored it and kept it as a virtual enclave, first within the terminal area, later within Point State Park, although the planners of the 1950s renewal wanted to remove it along with all other "old" buildings in the area.

Bouquet's Redoubt, 1764. Above: at the beginning of the 1890s. Left: as a D.A.R. enclave in Point State Park.

Like Bouquet's Redoubt, the Neill Log House of 1787 in Schenley Park was an extremely rare 18th-century survivor in the city. As with the Redoubt, a photographer or journalist might make occasional note of the "old-timer," yet nothing was done either to restore or preserve it. Landmarks took note of its presence, and in 1967 raised money for its restoration: none too soon, because as plans were going forward the house collapsed. Charles Morse Stotz, the restoration architect, disassembled it, numbered the logs for reassembly, and put it back together minus a large park storage addition to the rear.

The Redoubt and the Neill Log House were without architectural character, but their contact with the remotest past of the city gave them unique value. Admirable architecture, though, has had its own lucky escapes.

H. H. Richardson's Courthouse, finished in 1888, was one of the most admired and imitated buildings of

Neill Log House, Schenley Park, c. 1790. Below: in the early 1890s. Opposite, top: collapsed in 1967. Opposite, bottom: restored.

its time. Perhaps Richardson's main accomplishments were ignored: his ability to express a simple, logical plan in a picturesque form, his contrast of simple and visibly solid masonry with accents of ornament in a few telling places. Yet if nationwide imitations of isolated features of the Courthouse usually missed the essential points, they at least showed how greatly other architects were struck by the building. In 1904 the Courthouse was already hard-pressed to contain all the County facilities. Frederick John Osterling, himself a designer of wavering ability in Richardson Romanesque and a man short of modesty, proposed interpolating two extra stories in the Courthouse, raising the roof and the tower to fit. The

Allegheny County Buildings, downtown, 1884–88. Henry Hobson Richardson, architect. Right: as built. Above: early view of grand stair. Opposite, right, top: Osterling's proposal. Opposite, right, bottom: Hornbostel's proposal. Opposite, left: an A.I.A. compromise proposal of c. 1928, returning to the original cell-block plan but sacrificing Richardson's outer wall and chimney.

other architects of Pittsburgh rose against him, a jury for the Carnegie Museum of Art International volunteered their opinion on the idea—adverse—and the Bar Association decided, in addition, that it was not practical. The proposal failed, as did Henry Hornbostel's suggestion of 1907 for a skyscraper in the courtyard, and Judge Ellenbogen's that it simply be abandoned. The Courthouse has since undergone mediocre little alterations, but ones for the most part reversible.

The Jail has won more praise even than the Courthouse for its simple but subtle use of granite, and is probably Pittsburgh's only world-class building. Yet thus far it has been in serious danger of extinction twice. In 1924, downtown businessmen began a six-year campaign to eliminate such a gloomy and shameful place from the approach to their territory; architects and others spoke up for the Jail and its enclosing wall, and the matter died away. In 1954 the commercial threat was back, with Conrad Hilton interested in the site for a hotel and the County Commissioners apparently eager to sell. Once again there were protests against the demolition of the Jail, and these surely contributed to the abandonment of the idea though Hilton may have decided for his own reasons to look elsewhere. In 1972 and 1973, Landmarks had to defend the Jail, whose reputation *as* a jail was bad, against verbal attacks that could have led to a third threat. Now it must be defended again, in view of a mandated construction of a new Jail.

PUBLIC·BUILDING·GROUP·OF·ALLEGHENY·CO·
·ALTERED·AS·SUGGESTED·BY·THE·
·PITTSBURGH·CHAPTER·AMERICAN·INSTITUTE·OF·ARCHITECTS·

The terrain itself has had its perils. Cutting down the Hump in the Fifth Avenue and Grant Street areas was an expedient to make the Triangle street grid work; mitigation of the steep climb to Grant Street had been undertaken fitfully from 1836 until 1911-13, when the problem was finally solved. Nobody loved the Hump. But Junction Hollow, the ravine that separates the Carnegie Institute from the original Carnegie Tech campus, was surely another matter. In a way this tree-lined void spanned by the Schenley Bridge, 600 feet wide and 75 feet deep, sums up the contrasts of this city: grandeur in places, a casual coming-together of nature and man-made works elsewhere. There is a beauty in this wild space, a drama, that makes it something of a relief in the midst of so much that is built up, carefully cultivated, and parked on. Yet the Oakland Corporation in 1963 saw Junction Hollow as mere emptiness to be filled flush with laboratories, offices, and cultural institutions above an expressway. It perceived a manifest economic destiny in this seven-layered utilitarian structure, which would have extended from Forbes Avenue to Panther Hollow Lake. Lack of funds prevented it from coming to be, but the idea is occasionally revived.

Below: Reducing the Hump on Diamond Street, 1912 or 1913. Opposite: Junction Hollow, Oakland. Above: cross-section of the Oakland Corporation scheme. Below: Junction Hollow in 1989—something of a parking lot these days but still a deep space with wild growth on its slopes.

Above: the stadium over the Monongahela, replacing the Smithfield Street Bridge, making Station Square impossible, tunnelizing the river for 500 feet or more of its length. Below: houses, North Side slope.

A truly hideous meddling with nature, and one that shows utilitarianism at its purest, was the proposal of the 1950s to build Three Rivers Stadium not beside the Allegheny but *over* the Monongahela River, where it would have looked like a camping toilet. Ease of access and non-use of taxable land were claimed as conclusive reasons for tunnelizing the river.

Such architectural and topographic outrages would have been conspicuous, occurring in places often seen by the public. But neighborhoods too have been under threat, and in several cases the threat was fulfilled. Many of those who lived there may have seen them as mere shelter and have been indifferent to where they were living. Others, though, had held onto their dwellings tenaciously, improved them within their abilities, made friends, felt themselves at home, consciously or unconsciously enjoyed the familiar porches, walls, and roofs of their old buildings. These might have wished that their dwellings functioned better or that neighborhood life were more seemly, but a move to humane new housing would have disturbed the patterns of their lives. The City had the removal of hillside housing as part of its policy.

The North Side in the early 1950s was a blighted area, and there were figures to prove it. On the house fronts, peeling paint; behind the fronts, stenches, vermin, and too many people. Nothing in these decayed Victorian streets, surely, to think of as home; home was a bright economic future with material well-being.

The origin of Landmarks has long taken on a legendary character. In early 1964, James D. Van Trump and Arthur P. Ziegler, Jr. were walking along the 1300 block of Liverpool Street in Manchester, looking at a remarkable row of mansard-roofed double houses and deploring a condition that foretold their replacement by new housing. The idea came to them of a preservation group that would find means of continuing such houses in use, externally restored, fully habitable, and with the same kinds of people, if not exactly the same people, in each house. More public buildings too would be saved. Such preservation would have to prove itself to officials and money sources, and to the neighborhoods themselves. The Pittsburgh History & Landmarks Foundation was incorporated on September 30, 1964, and in time gained credibility as an organization with practical and considerate alternatives to conventional urban renewal.

In Manchester, beginning in 1965, Landmarks formed a working relationship with the City's Urban Redevelopment Authority, and raised a mixture of government and private money. It later worked with the Manchester Citizens Corporation, whose name states its constituency, and set up a marketing campaign to attract new inhabitants and increase neighborhood pride and prestige in order to retain existing residents: the first such preservation program in the nation. In the latter connection, entry of most of Manchester on the National Register of Historic Places in 1975 was of great help, although the City Planning Department opposed the effort for years.

Manchester, North Side. Left: 1300 block of Liverpool Street in sad times. Above: demonstrating enthusiasm for life in Manchester.

A plan of 1954, not official and not detailed but certainly suggestive, showed almost everything in the nearby Mexican War Streets replaced by uniform garden apartments. The modest layout of 1854 on what had been farmland had developed into a setting for pleasant middle-class Mid- and Late-Victorian houses with a few stores and churches; but here too blight had long set in. Landmarks, coming here in 1966, varied its Manchester practices by buying and rehabilitating houses to set an example, which bit by bit was followed. Manchester had been mainly black, but in the Mexican War Streets a mixture of races and of incomes was the ideal pursued, though once again with the very minimum of displacement.

North Side above North Avenue, 1954. Below: actuality. Bottom: vision.

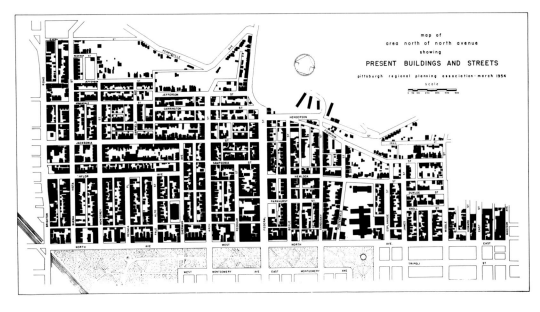

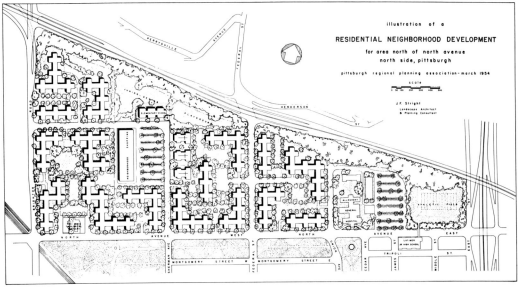

Mexican War Streets, North Side. Left: 1233 Resaca Place, restored. Below: 1200 block, Buena Vista Street, after some work was done. Bottom: 1200 block, Resaca Place.

Elsewhere on the North Side a few individual buildings, originally not considered for preservation, were saved. When the buildings of the old Allegheny Town within the Commons were razed for Allegheny Center, the old Post Office, on Ohio Street next to the Buhl Planetarium, got a respite. It was to come down, however, and in 1967 *Landmark Architecture of Allegheny County* flatly called it "doomed." But Landmarks was in fact not quite ready to give up, feeling that this was a handsome building and a valuable feature linking the utilitarian 1960s to the neighborhood's past. 1968 saw negotiations with the Urban Redevelopment Authority and plans to re-use the building as Landmarks' home and as a museum of local history. The negotiations, laborious though they were, succeeded; the master plan was altered, and the Old Post Office Museum opened in 1971. Its interior was enriched with salvaged decorative work from Ridge Avenue houses that had come down a few years before.

Old Post Office, Allegheny (North Side), 1897. William Martin Aiken, architect. Below: in the 1930s. Opposite, below: under conversion into the Old Post Office Museum, c. 1970. Opposite, left, above: repairs, 1980. Opposite, right, above: detail from the Post Office screen, now removed.

Anderson Monument, 1904, North Side. Daniel Chester French, sculptor; Henry Bacon, architect. Above: as restored, against the Buhl Science Center. Below: as originally built.

The library in Allegheny, situated at the same Ohio and Federal intersection where the Planetarium and the now-gone Market House stood, was the first of the many built by Andrew Carnegie. Though not a distinguished building it was literally a landmark, with a tall tower marking the old crossroads, and thus something to be saved. In the early 1970s, moved by a Landmarks-neighborhood campaign and a 7,000-signature petition, the City committed itself to restoration of the building. "Restoration" was a relative term, for within the cleaned exterior the spaces are now quite different from their original state, while Carnegie's memorial to Colonel James Anderson, who helped in his early education, was dispersed, its bronze sculptures put in separate places and the granite work destroyed. In 1988, nearly two decades later, the Anderson Monument was fully restored.

St. Mary's Church and Priory were within the take line of the I-279 project that destroyed most of central Dutchtown, and were acquired by PennDot in 1973 to afford room for an interchange ramp. The next year, however, the buildings were found to be National Register-eligible; this meant that Federal money, which was supplying 90 percent of the highway construction funds, could not be used to destroy the St. Mary's group without a clear case of necessity. PennDot redesigned the ramp, and put the buildings up for sale in 1983; a preservation covenant was to be included in the deed. The buildings were purchased, with Landmarks, the North Side Civic Development Council, and the East Allegheny Community Council aiding in the conversion of the priory into a bed-and-breakfast inn of the same name. The church is to be converted into a public rental hall as soon as parking requirements are met.

St. Mary's Church and Priory, Dutchtown, 1854 and 1888. Above: with the original onion domes, in a view from the 1930s. Below: restored Priory front. Below, left: courtyard.

The East Street Valley Expressway, the northern arm of I-279, menaced St. Boniface's Roman Catholic Church to the extent that, in 1975, Landmarks was about to despair. Farther Ambrose and parishioners had been protesting the demolition, and in 1970, Landmarks joined them. Mayor Flaherty was of great help in his demands that the church, then in PennDot hands, be bypassed. The church was offered again to the Diocese, the plans having been revised in such a way that the church need not go, but the Diocese preferred to let it go. Pressure on the Diocese continued, and by 1977 the mood was cautiously optimistic. The situation was eventually reversed, and St. Boniface still functions as a parish church along a length of road where no other buildings exist.

St. Boniface Church, East Street Valley, 1926. A. F. Link, architect. Left: front in the 1970s. Below and opposite: interiors, as photographed when the church was new.

This same utilitarian spirit has threatened historic places outside Pittsburgh. Mann's Hotel in McKees Rocks dates in part from the beginning of the 19th century, and in part from successive building campaigns of 1855 and 1895. The pride of the hotel is its 1900-period barroom, plain, old-fashioned, heated only by a coal stove. The building is a cumulative affair, bearing the signs of its numerous growths and conversions without regard to period. In 1979 a realigned reconstruction of the Windgap Bridge threatened to remove the Hotel. Landmarks aided in a protest that went all the way to Washington, D.C., and the alignment of the new bridge was changed so as to spare Mann's Hotel.

In 1970 the Burtner house in Harrison Township was in danger from a nearby State highway project, as plans called for a temporary right-of-way, and then an interchange, on its site. Landmarks worked with a local preservation committee to prevail on the Pennsylvania Department of Highways to save the house: which they did at the last minute, while the demolition crew was on its way. Since then, Landmarks has assisted an independent preservation group in restoration of the house.

Mann's Hotel, McKees Rocks, c. 1810 and after. Bottom: front. Below: barroom.

Burtner house, Harrison Township. Below: beset by roads, c. 1970. Left: as restored, c. 1980.

"Woodville," the Neville house in Collier Township, was under several threats in the early 1970s. The 200-year-old house itself was no longer occupied, and its grounds, already reduced to the immediate house area, were threatened with both road construction and a flood-control project for Chartiers Creek, and were offered for sale. In 1974 Landmarks met with the Army Corps of Engineers and worked out a waterfall-like formation of concrete for the creek alongside the house. In 1976, Landmarks began a campaign to buy the property, and soon did so. The Neville House Auxiliary, formed two years later, undertook the restoration, which is still in progress. In 1987, Landmarks formed the Neville House Advisory Committee, whose volunteer members were professional interior decorators, historians, architects, and archaeologists. With funding support from Landmarks and the Allegheny Committee of the National Society of Colonial Dames of America, the Neville House Advisory Committee has restored, redecorated, and refurnished the living room, dining room, and hallway according to their 18th-century condition. Archaeologists have found evidence of prehistoric dwellings on the site, while architectural historians have puzzled out the complicated history of the house, with its many additions and changes. The Neville house is the most significant 18th-century house in Allegheny County, and one of five National Historic Landmarks in the County.

"Woodville," Collier Township, c. 1785 and after. Below: exterior as restored. Opposite, top: dining room as restored. Opposite, bottom: exterior after early preservation work.

Not only old neighborhoods and rural places but the buildings and land of large railroad stations have seemed to invite demolition and rebuilding. In the 1960s, passenger railroad travel looked like a thing of the past except on a very few heavily-traveled lines. The many station tracks were unneeded, and so were the pompous waiting rooms built for hundreds. There were, at least tentatively, other uses for the land.

The Pittsburgh & Lake Erie station complex, on the south shore of the Monongahela River opposite the Golden Triangle, offered Landmarks an even greater challenge in the early 1970s than its earlier projects had done. The railroad had expanded its buildings and trackage over 42 acres by 1930, but after three decades its need for the facilities had so declined that the land seemed a vacuum into which new development would rush. In the late 1960s there was talk of a Mon Plaza that would replace everything. Landmarks offered an opposing plan to save the Terminal for restaurant purposes, but by the mid-1970s its plan for the conversion of the whole P&LE property into Station Square was roughed out, and both the public in general and those who could help the project were being solicited. Landmarks signed a lease for the property, effective in 1976, and 1977 through 1984 saw the historic property rehabilitated and occupied by a mixture of business and retail operations. Of the buildings already gone when Landmarks arrived, only two were prominent. A trolley shelter in front of the passenger station, torn down in 1967 over Landmarks' objections, was a regrettable loss; the 700-foot balloon trainshed, gone since 1935, would have been a remarkable structure but one hardly usable

and a block to the river view that is one of Station Square's prides. Five other buildings from the years 1897 to 1917 are now in continuing use, and the property is a refuge for architectural fragments and industrial artifacts that tell of the region's past. Development is continuing on an area of land, now 52 acres, that the conventional wisdom once found too remote from the Triangle to succeed.

Station Square (Pittsburgh & Lake Erie Railroad Station), built 1897–1984. Left: passenger station of 1901 as built. Below: station with the trolley shelter of 1912. Opposite, above: passenger waiting room. Opposite, below: Mon Plaza.

The fourth Union Station, by the late 1960s, was a redundant building. It had been built as a major transfer point and as a railroad office building, but in 1968 the Penn Central Transportation Company, which had gone in heavily for diversification, had plans to tear down everything for a commercial development called Penn Central Park. By 1970, partly because of Landmarks' publicizing of the matter, the architects found means to save at least the "rotunda," the fantastic Beaux-Arts shelter over the carriage turning circle that was then functioning, in an improvised way, as a Trailways bus stop. Nothing but deterioration happened in the next decade and a half. Landmarks did a survey of Union Station in 1977 and concluded that it would do well as a hotel and made an offer, rejected by the City, to develop it as such. Proposals and developers came and went, with no practical results. Passenger train service was eventually revived on a very limited basis from a station improvised behind the building. In 1985, Historic Landmarks for Living, a Philadelphia developer with experience in large-building rehabilitation, restored the exterior and the waiting room, and made the rest over into the Pennsylvanian apartment house.

Union Station, downtown, 1902. D. H. Burnham & Co., architects. Below: Penn Central Park. Bottom: early 20th-century view.

Left: Union Station waiting room in its last days of use—a blacked-out skylight over a canopy lighting a new ticket enclosure. Above: waiting room under restoration, summer of 1989.

Eberhardt and Ober Brewery, Dutchtown, c. 1880 and after. Architects unknown. Below: the brewery neglected. Above: the brewery restored.

Besides places that might have fallen victim to positive development plans there are others that would in the ordinary course of things have been lost since there seemed no point in keeping them; they were too little wanted it seemed, had outlived their usefulness. And yet people got together and found means of saving them.

The Eberhardt and Ober brewery buildings, at the foot of Troy Hill, exemplified an economic vacuum which, sooner or later, something new would have filled. They were underused and deserted for years, and with no suitable future use in sight they would sooner or later have been taken down as had other brewery buildings near by. In 1986, though, a feasibility study was done, indicating that a mixture of new uses would work in the buildings. The North Side Civic Development Council and other organizations undertook the project, whose principal tenant was to include a microbrewery. Landmarks' Preservation Fund was one of the financing sources of the project, whose formal opening was in the fall of 1988.

The Byers-Lyon house had survived the demolitions of the late 1960s by the Community College of Allegheny County that had taken out a half-dozen adjoining Ridge Avenue houses. This did not, however, imply a commitment of the College to save this double mansion. In 1972 it seemed that the time was up, and that the site would become a parking lot. Landmarks wrote a reproachful letter to the County Commissioners protesting the demolitions that had happened, and especially this imminent one. As a result the College agreed not to destroy the house, which kept on for 16 years more, not threatened but in rather indifferent condition. In 1988 it underwent a complete facade and partial interior restoration for use as a student activities center, and now the Community College is very proud of its historic building.

Byers-Lyon house, Ridge Avenue, 1898. Alden & Harlow, architects. After restoration.

The East Liberty Market House has been not only a farmers' market but a sports arena, trade-show hall, and automobile showroom, serving in the last role until about 1980. The interior space was obviously adaptable to a number of functions but was also large, and the building stood in a commercial area that was making but a slow recovery from a period of bad decline. Underused or unused, it might well have been torn down in time. In 1986, however, the Massaro Corporation announced its intention of remodeling the building as a shopping center. Landmarks Design Associates produced a plan that satisfied National Register standards while offering three levels of shopping. Motor Square Garden—the building had long been known by this name—reopened in 1988.

Motor Square Garden, East Liberty, 1900. Peabody & Stearns, architects; Landmarks Design Associates, architects for adaptation. Below and opposite, top: interiors as they now are. Opposite, bottom: exterior before restoration.

St. Anthony's Chapel on Troy Hill was a private creation of Father Suibertus Mollinger, parish priest of the Most Holy Name of Jesus. Into it he had put 5,000 relics. By 1972 the chapel was dirty and in bad repair, but in that year Mary Wohleber, a Landmarks' board member, initiated a private campaign that in under two years raised enough donations to secure and restore the exterior; no parish money was used, and no money was borrowed. Restoration was completed in 1977, and an adjoining museum opened in 1986.

St. Anthony's Chapel, Troy Hill, 1880 and 1892. Architects unknown.

St. Luke's Episcopal Church in Scott Township stands on ground used for Anglican worship since 1765, but in this century the church has been used intermittently, and by 1955 it had deteriorated to the point that it could not be used at all. A new roof structure secured the fabric, yet nothing major was done other than that for two decades. In 1975 the Diocese convened a committee to remedy the situation; in 1977 this became the St. Luke's Auxiliary of Landmarks. By 1982, with Landmarks' advice and contribution of work-crew labor and volunteers from Old St. Luke's, the situation was notably better, and by the end of 1987 the church was being used ecumenically for occasional services, weddings, concerts, and meetings.

St. Luke's Episcopal Church (Old St. Luke's), Woodville, Scott Township. Architect unknown. Exterior and interior as restored.

The Braddock Carnegie Library had undergone the same dangers as those that destroyed the Carnegie Library at Duquesne—a lost endowment and a transfer to a local School Board unwilling or unable to keep it in use. The County intervened to the extent of calling in Landmarks, in 1974, to do a feasibility study on the closed and much-deteriorated building; this concluded that adaptive use for a variety of community functions was practicable. In 1983 the Braddock's Field Historical Society assumed ownership, and kept the library portion of the multi-use building at least partly open. Five years later, partial repairs and some new interior construction had been done, and money was coming in for complete rehabilitation at an increasing rate.

Braddock Carnegie Library, Braddock, 1888. William Halsey Wood, architect. Enlarged, 1893; Longfellow, Alden & Harlow, architects. Before rehabilitation.

The Duquesne Heights Incline, scaling Mount Washington opposite the Point, is the newer of the two surviving Pittsburgh inclines, yet retains its track structure and its cars of 1877. In 1962 the Incline was closed after an accident; at the time it had been running at a large loss. Local citizens did not want to lose it, however, and in 1963 the Society for the Preservation of the Duquesne Incline undertook full responsibility, renting the Incline for a dollar a year from Port Authority Transit. The Society repaired the working parts, restored the Eastlake interiors of the cars and the Victorian upper station, and took over the operations. In 1988 they enlarged the upper station and added an observation platform from which visitors can look for miles along the three river valleys.

Duquesne Incline, Duquesne Heights to Station Square, 1877. Samuel Diescher, engineer. Above: Duquesne Heights station as enlarged. Below: Eastlake car interior of 1877.

*1417 East Carson Street, South Side, c. 1880.
Architect unknown. Above: before restoration.
Right: as restored.*

General trends, mostly well-intentioned, have at times threatened to mar the character of a neighborhood, and here the problem was not to modify a master plan or rescue something neglected, but rather to secure the future of something in continuing use.

The South Side, and Carson Street in particular, was a handsome neighborhood in the mid-1960s, a collection of commercial and residential buildings that had kept a small-town quality though the skyscrapers of the Triangle were visible a mile away. As a neighborhood and as an architectural accumulation, though, the South Side was in trouble. The population was growing older and the Carson Street stores and apartments were underused, partly because a light-industrial rezoning of much of the area in 1958 had discouraged habitation and lessened the economic base for the stores. A return to residential zoning in 1966 had restored morale, but resulting local efforts to fix up buildings ignored the character of what the neighborhood had to offer. Begin-

ning in 1968, Landmarks initiated a restoration program
that stressed that the prevailing Mid- and Late-Victorian architecture was a positive asset to the community.
The Chamber of Commerce, the Community Council,
and later the Birmingham Union, founded in 1976, came
out solidly in favor of this attitude toward the slow
recovery that was occurring. Further encouragement to
restoration and preservation came in 1983 with the
naming of Carson Street as a National Register District,
and in 1985, when the National Trust made Carson
Street its first urban Main Street, beneficiary of three
years of counseling on everything from architectural
restoration to merchandising. The South Side Local
Development Corporation and other community organizations have been continuing the work. There is
much yet to do, and one facade alteration of 1988 seems
to have been done literally in spite of preservationist
intentions, but Carson Street and the South Side generally are looking better than they did 20 years ago.

*1701–13 East Carson Street, South Side. Below: view, c.
1980. Above: Number 1707 as altered, summer of 1988.*

We of this area have had some happy escapes, partly because of blind chance, mostly because people united, protested a proposed demolition, worked out a plan for continuing use. Landmarks has been in on many of the preservation campaigns, with leadership, ideas, facts, financial help, and liaison with those who can cause change and those who undergo the consequences of change. Beginning in the 1980s Landmarks strengthened its historic preservation effort by developing an education department. Through publications, tours, student-teacher workshops, and special events Landmarks creates an awareness of local history and its visible signs, the landmarks. With such education, preservation comes to be seen as a serious possibility, an option to be considered with regard to a building or place left to us from the past.

Imagine: a badly distorted Courthouse, and a big, bland hotel in place of the Jail; a parking lot instead of a mansion; a traffic ramp instead of the Priory; empty land where Motor Square Garden or the Eberhardt and Ober Brewery stood; Allegheny Center covering all of the North Side; flat 1960s landscaping over a disappeared ravine. Places valued by us might have been lost, given no voice raised in time.

Another view of the Oakland Corporation's Junction Hollow plan. Carnegie Institute is at the upper right, Panther Hollow Lake at the lower right. Opposite, above: Eberhardt and Ober Brewery restored. Opposite, below: Union Station rotunda restored.

What May Be Kept

The twenty-fifth anniversary of an organization such as ours, diversely experienced and with more work to come, offers an occasion, or perhaps a pretext, for examining the whole matter of "historic preservation," its philosophy, its role, and its possible scope. It also is an occasion to look at Pittsburgh and its surrounding region, make some effort to outline what is generally distinctive about it and deserving to be preserved whatever the future brings. Finally, it is an occasion to consider Landmarks and what its work may be in the future.

Creative Preservation

To begin with, we may well examine history itself from the preservationist's viewpoint. It is wrong to see history in a merely retrospective way, conceive of it only as an affair of things that have happened. The past and the future are like a cable formed from strands of varying length and prominence that overlap so that, barring some violent severing, they form a continuity regardless of wherever individual strands may end or begin. True preservation will understand this. To most of us, Pittsburgh is home. Things change, in our own little world as individuals, family members, or residents of a neighborhood, and in the larger world of the whole city. Much of the change is at least acceptable, some of it is positively desirable, and if we are lucky the changes are not so radical that we become disoriented and wonder where our home has gone. Preservation, properly understood, understands that there *will* be a future and seeks to integrate with this future those things from the past that have been especially good and familiar and beautiful: specific buildings and other places in some

Above: architectural patterns, historical overlaps. Opposite: Liverpool Street, Manchester.

79

instances; in other instances ways of building, of using the land, general characteristics of the physical environment that are the preservationist's special domain.

It has to be understood, of course, that the physical character of a community is only one element, if a major one, that exists in interaction with other elements, social and economic especially, that make up the whole community as its citizens perceive it. We build and make use of land to accommodate certain ways of living and working, and as these change, so may we have to build in new ways.

"Historic preservation" needs to examine its conscience. It can offer valid reasons for many of its individual campaigns: In this place, history is made concrete, has a physical presence: here the great man's character was formed, here the great event took place, here a way of life, an industrial process, something of the sort is still vividly presented. This building or this landscape is too beautiful to destroy. This place is so intimately associated with our community that what is fine and distinctive about the community would be diminished if it went. This building has qualities of space, ornamentation, workmanship that people prize and that modern construction does not afford. With a little imagination this other building need not be torn down, since it is adaptable to modern needs. Such arguments may well apply in individual instances. Yet there is a danger of artificiality and contrivance about conventional historic preservation, of forced make-believe, just as there was danger from starry-eyed money-chasing or standardized do-gooding in the conventional urban renewal that historic preservation arose, as a major force, to combat. The preservationist must not drag his protected structures into the future, there to drift as indigestible lumps in a world to which they have no relevance, for some vaguely-conceived "ever after."

Rather, he must know that what he will fight to protect has a place and a meaning in the future. There are very few Parthenons, pure monuments whose very artistry and public significance are clinching arguments for their preservation. Most of the buildings, neighborhoods, and other places preservationists attempt to save were built, however carefully and with whatever artistry, on a produce-or-die basis, and in the natural course of events they would ultimately disappear. And really, if you look at the buildings preservationists have

We do have pure monuments, whose very existence is the reason for their existence; their messages to the public and their artistry constitute their purpose.

Most of what Man builds is seen fundamentally as a means to an end. When that end or some subsequent purpose for the structure is no longer adequately served, its demolition is in sight. In the meantime it may have undergone remodelings, typically for the worse. When most buildings come down the regrets are few. Here and there, though, a place is the focus of so many people's memories that it is one of the unofficial institutions of the community. It is usually commercial in nature, but it has such a style about it that people seek it out and later remember it fondly. As such places disappear, one may hope that other places—or something of some sort—are coming along to become institutions of the modern community.

Above: George Westinghouse Memorial, Schenley Park, 1930. Henry Hornbostel and Eric Fisher Wood, architects; Daniel Chester French and Paul Fjelde, sculptors. Left: Norse Room, Fort Pitt Hotel, 1909–67. Janssen & Abbott, architects.

Just a reminder: in 1968 it looked as if we were to lose Union Station and gain Penn Central Park.

In central Allegheny we did not preserve and rehabilitate; we built anew.

campaigned to save, most are mediocre in both architecture and history. The suspicion inevitably arises that historic preservation, given its prevalence in the last two decades or so, is largely a vote of No Confidence in modern architecture, planning, and development. And not a mistaken vote either. We have had some big and awful things imposed on us, other ones threatened, and much small-scale mediocrity placed along our streets. In the opinion of this author, architecture has been in a state of upset for 150 years, trying to cope with unfamiliar design problems, agonizing over matters of style, and yet attempting now and then a unilateral solution to the world's problems. We *have* had masterpieces, developed some good vernaculars, created some very agree-

Two houses in central Allegheny, now gone.

able neighborhoods: and still we have not quite found assurance that the designer's hand was a good hand to be in.

Historic preservation, then, appears these days to go beyond the saving of specific buildings and other places for specific, positive reasons. It is a reactionary movement, literally, a defence against drab, dumb construction of the sort all too likely to happen or against, indeed, the coming-to-be of yet another parking lot where at least passable architecture has stood. But we should be doing what we can to see that there is no cultural need to preserve less than the most distinguished places from the past. Our ideal should be a state of things in which we can anticipate new works of building, planning, and development with confidence that they will be at least as beautiful and heart-warming as what they replace.

What one can normally expect from an ordinary builder is quite different now from what it was a century or two ago.

Miller house, South Park, 1808 and 1830.

Even if such a negative view of the present preservation movement is right, the preservationist remains a specialized, perhaps blinkered, ally of all those who are concerned with the "quality of life." Perhaps he needs to turn around and look, with these others, into the future. His community, unless it is very unlucky, has developed special excellences, of which those of the physical environment with which he is concerned are one element. Some of the excellences he knows are specifically related to extant buildings. Others can be abstracted from the whole mass of existing architecture and place-making of all sorts and, liberated from surface matters of style and period, be used to influence new building, planning, and development. True preservation lets the city change, but change so that all the essential good of the past is saved, even augmented, and new building is welcomed on the condition that this happens.

The preservationist should thus concern himself with what is to be built as well as what has to be kept. His knowledge and his interests will be limited, but within his limits he can be a scholar, an ideologue, and a propagandist in a general movement to maintain and improve a community that continues to be home to its inhabitants.

It is hard to find Pittsburgh examples of self-assured, tasteful but no-nonsense modern design, but these two restaurant interiors show such design in a milieu where utter plainness or contrived fakery is the norm.

Above: Le Petit Cafe, Shadyside, 1983. L.P. Perfido Associates, architects. Below: Cafe Stephen B., 1978. Arthur Lubetz Associates, architects.

Strict preservation is not always best. It can be argued that these three buildings were actually improved by remodelings, done in two instances after fires.

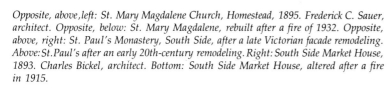

Opposite, above,left: St. Mary Magdalene Church, Homestead, 1895. Frederick C. Sauer, architect. Opposite, below: St. Mary Magdalene, rebuilt after a fire of 1932. Opposite, above, right: St. Paul's Monastery, South Side, after a late Victorian facade remodeling. Above:St.Paul's after an early 20th-century remodeling. Right: South Side Market House, 1893. Charles Bickel, architect. Bottom: South Side Market House, altered after a fire in 1915.

In Our Case

In our case, the visual, material character of the community derives mostly from the dramatic, ambivalent relationship of Man and Nature. The physical geography that provided westward-flowing rivers and seams of coal gave Pittsburgh a reason for coming to be and a reason for growing steadily. That same geography, though, resisted the growth, prevented solid city-wide concentrations of building, scattered construction over the rolling landscape, necessitated great engineering works. It stimulated the works of Man, attacked them, frustrated them, and prevented them from being obsessedly tidy let alone grandiose. Man attacked Nature

not only with his retaining walls and pavements but through the fumes of his industrial plants. At present, Nature, patient and opportunistic, is invading the very furnaces now that they are cold.

Nature has been undoubtedly lavish with us, at least, in providing great spaces and spectacular views, a place in three dimensions one never tires of seeing. Annoyance and danger are the penalties for a city living on so many levels, but there is as recompense this wonderful spatial endowment.

Of architecture we do indeed have handsome examples, just as we have our monuments and our structures and places that there is reason to preserve. But apart from a few isolated places, the continuing visual character of Pittsburgh will depend on a sense of Man in

The Pittsburgh region is founded on the delta of a long-gone river of 300,000,000 years ago, eroded as much as 500 feet deep by the present river system, which is about 12,000 years old. People of European origin have been in the area about 250 years.

Bluffs at Mile 13 on the Monongahela, opposite the Duquesne Works.

the terrain, the way he builds, the means he uses to impose his will on the stubborn contours of the land. The architecture of the future, which can perpetuate or mar this visual character, will depend on the demands of the evolving social and economic character of the community; and the ways in which we build and in which we occupy the land may alter to meet the new demands. We must be ready, maintaining continuity in the midst of change.

In the last 250 years, Pittsburghers have learned to tame the terrain somewhat, get over and around it, mine its coal, navigate its rivers. They have had to create engineering works, some of them handsome and large, to move people, goods, and utilities.

Opposite: south portal of the Liberty Tunnels in 1932. Left: Knoxville Incline, 1890–1961. Below: the Point in the 1960s.

Man and Nature have had an uneasy coexistence around Pittsburgh. When heavy industry flourished, its structure rivaled the hills themselves for prominence on the scene. Nature in the form of vegetation withdrew entirely in some places, as it did at Hazelwood when the beehive coke ovens poisoned the air. But Nature was always waiting to come back, always sneaking in an ailanthus or a clump of weeds in some untraveled part of the industrial property, and now that the industrial plants are so largely shut down it is reveling among the ponderous machines and even within the vast sheds.

Opposite, above: Pittsburgh Works, Jones & Laughlin, in 1974. Opposite, below: Hazelwood in 1907. Left: Duquesne Works, 1987. Below: Hazelwood coke plant, Jones & Laughlin, in the 1960s.

There are large river plain and upland plateau areas in the city, where buildings stand side by side in orderly grids of streets. There are imposing architectural groups here and there. But there has never been a grand boulevard, and hardly ever a grand square, on the Parisian model. Even tidy urbanistic treatments on a smaller scale are frustrated in many places because of the terrain. Narrow streets wind along the hillsides and in the ravines, sometimes reaching a thoroughfare in due course, sometimes ending abruptly at a cross street as narrow as themselves or at some climbing or plunging surface of land that is patently too steep to travel. Here, steps of wood or concrete sometimes take over. This is in many places, perforce, a casual city, resistant to neat techniques of settlement.

Opposite, above: Junction Hollow, Oakland. Opposite, below: Vinecliffe Street, Mount Washington. Below: house probably now gone, on the edge of the East Street Valley.

Yet this casual city is wonderful to see. As architecture the buildings are humdrum, but they are so dispersed as to articulate the surfaces of the land. Close up, they accentuate the rise and fall of their streets; far away, they are like brushstrokes on a landscape painting, indistinct forms whose smallness shows how distant they are. Standing on a height in this three-dimensional city, you can see remote neighborhoods, not merely a portion of your own.

Opposite: Kearsarge Street, Mount Washington, looking south. Left and below: houses on the South Side slopes.

The typical building of Pittsburgh is still the single-family house, whose modest dimensions are in no visual conflict with the landscape. Now and then a church, a school, an engineering work, or a commercial center breaks out of this matrix of houses with its larger bulk and more elaborate architecture. The houses, built under differing circumstances—terrain, lot size, and wealth of family, time of construction, architectural style—often conform to others in their neighborhoods yet display a great variety citywide, so that a glance at a picture of one often suffices for a good guess at where its subject stands.

Opposite: South Side slopes below St. Paul's Monastery. Right: St. Michael Archangel Church, South Side. Below: Vallonia Street, West End.

Below, left: houses on Beechwood Boulevard. Below, right: house on the South Side. Bottom: duplexes on Forward Avenue, Squirrel Hill. Opposite: house formerly under the East Street Bridge.

Aside from the hillside houses with their stilt-like basements, there is nothing distinctively Pittsburgh about the actual buildings. The city originated no architectural styles and unique techniques of construction or planning, though notice must be taken of the originality of Frederick G. Scheibler, Jr., as an architect and of the early application of several innovations in bridge construction. The pre-Renaissance city we still largely inhabit has come to us with a dual architectural identity typical of American cities that developed from the mid-19th through the early 20th centuries. Its older architecture, that of the time when Pittsburgh was still the Iron city, is Victorian, small-scale in treatment, rather obsessed with decorative details in isolation, hard-surfaced, hard-edged, unsubtle in its choice of materials which, realistically enough in our atmosphere, were inclined to be dark.

Left: cast-iron front, formerly downtown, c. 1870. Below: B.F. Jones house, Brighton Road, c. 1880–1955. Opposite, above: Bloomfield Bridge, 1914–c. 1978. Opposite, below: Spencer house, Amberson Avenue, Shadyside, 1886. George S. Orth, architect.

First National Bank, downtown, 1871. Architect unknown.

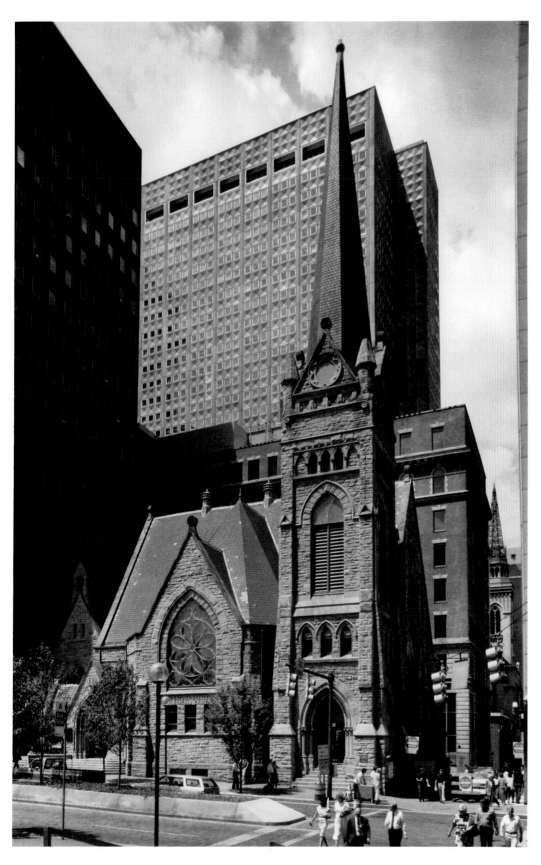

First Lutheran Church, downtown, 1887. Andrew Peebles, architect.

H. H. Richardson's County Buildings, finished in 1888, were an early beginning of a newer architecture, in which the building as a whole composition received more attention, with decorative details subordinated to the overall effect and sometimes even eliminated. Color and texture were subtly used, especially in house construction, and aside from rich Romantic effects in brick or fieldstone the trend was toward light-colored materials such as terra cotta, pale granite, and limestone. Pittsburgh soot was ignored in this newer, more sophisticated architecture, often by famous architects from outside the city and typically built in Oakland, the East End, and the suburbs, away from the industrial valleys.

Opposite, above: portals, Courthouse, as originally built. Opposite, below: Moreland-Hoffstot house, Shadyside, 1914. Paul Irwin, architect. Left: First Baptist Church, Oakland, 1911. Bertram Grosvenor Goodhue, architect. Below: Chatham Village, Mount Washington, 1931 and 1935. Ingham & Boyd, architects.

Right: terra-cotta details, Maul Building, 1910, South Side. William G. Wilkins Co., architects. Below: Washington Crossing Bridge, Allegheny River, 1923. Charles S. Davis, engineer; Janssen & Cocken, architects. Opposite: Frick Building, downtown, 1902. D.H. Burnham & Co., architects.

If in most neighborhoods the houses created a matrix that larger structures varied rather than violated, a number of very large buildings have made emphatic breaks with their surroundings, imposing their own images rather than conforming to the prevailing tone. Often the public has been able to accept this because these non-conforming structures, through a mixture of visual quality and public significance, have a special air of authority. The Cathedral of Learning, rising over humble buildings and among buildings of equal elegance but very different in style, proportions, and height, was not only a beautiful if absurd tower but was consciously intended to point the way to a better life through education. The promise and the importance of education seem to give some of our schools, such as South Hills High School, rightful positions on the hilltops. The East Liberty Presbyterian Church might be considered presumptuous; it has the air of a cathedral though it houses but one religious denomination among many: but it is the fifth such church to mark the old village crossroads since 1819. A steel plant lacks such elegance of form or idealism of purpose, but the town whose horizon its roofs and chimneys form was brought into being by this plant. It has been a supreme fact in the lives of the inhabitants. It may be added that, as well as being inescapably visible, a functioning steel plant has its own visual fascinations and its own beauty. Here, too, is authority.

Opposite: the Cathedral of Learning (1936–37; Charles Z. Klauder, architect) from Juliet Street, South Oakland. Below: the Liberty Tunnels Ventilator Plant (1928; Stanley L. Roush, architect) and South Hills High School (1924; Alden & Harlow, architects), on the rear slope of Mount Washington.

Below: East Liberty Presbyterian Church (1935; Cram & Ferguson, architects) from South Highland Avenue. Opposite: Duquesne, Pa. and the Duquesne Works, U.S. Steel Corporation, before 1968.

Such are the elements of a good visual legacy that we may hope to perpetuate in ways that respond to changing future conditions. We have legacies not so good. Seldom have we designed an ordinary house that was genuinely satisfying to look at as a work of art. We have created some highly visible and stupid buildings and building complexes in the name of progress and development. We have created some genuine messes in the McKnight Road manner. Despite its present picturesque details, our city needs to be improved as a functioning mechanism, and the Veterans' Bridge and I-279 show how unfeelingly we now attack the larger aspects of the problem. Our modernization attempts in the past have offended the eyes with painted brickwork, applied shakes, fake shutters, and the conspicuous absence of many front porches. We should be able to do better, and unless we wish gradually to give up the use of our eyes except as informational and navigational devices we will have to do better. An understanding of what is good in that which we have now is the way to begin.

Below: a Munhall street. Opposite, above: South Side and Oakland, from St. Paul's Monastery. Opposite, below: Westinghouse Bridge, Turtle Creek, 1930. Allegheny County Department of Public Works, engineers.

Landmarks Looks Ahead

Trying to see a quarter-century into the future is too much; a decade is more reasonable for an organization such as Landmarks, whose diversified programs should respond to major historic change as it appears.

In the matter of "creative preservation" as outlined above, we foresee that we will demand and encourage excellence in architecture, planning, and development, not by laying down universal design rules or principles but through advocacy based on our experience of local architecture and of the terrain itself. We intend neither to be abstract and theoretical in our attitudes to specific problems nor to approve of architects and planners being so; rather, we will encourage response to both the specific requirements of a problem and the character of the environment.

Such advocacy is best done with the backing of a public that appreciates the history, the character, and the culture of the region in which it lives. We will continue to offer education that will spell out these matters in detail, and continue to impart pleasure and pride in and a deeper understanding of this remarkable place that is our home. Tours will show the reality; lectures, exhibits, television programs, and school curricula will impart ideas; publications will give information in a permanent form. Without public understanding and support there is not much meaning to what we do, and thus our educational program, the way in which we make our intentions best known, will have to continue vigorous, imaginative, and diversified.

On our own and in collaboration with others, we will preserve certain places and artifacts that vividly recall our early history or that are major works of public art. In addition to properties like the Neville house, Old St. Luke's, and the Allegheny Post Office with which we have been long associated, we are at the beginning of two grand permanent displays of the technological past at Station Square: an expanded Transportation Mu-

Landmarks educational activities. Below: taking a tombstone rubbing on a City Safari. Bottom: embroidering a design at Landmarks' Hands-On History Festival. Opposite, above: a teacher in-service. Opposite, below: student exhibitors at the Hands-On History Festival.

Above: a tour group at the First Presbyterian Church. Opposite, above: Steel Industry Heritage Task Force at Carrie Furnaces. Opposite, below: Landmarks publications.

seum and a Riverside Industrial Walk along which vivid objects from heavy industry in the Pittsburgh area will stand. Furthermore, as participants of the Steel Industry Heritage Task Force, we are currently trying to preserve for the public Carrie Furnaces Nos. 6 and 7 and the Pinkerton landing site of the Homestead Works. Our success in so doing is still uncertain, but so is the point at which such industrial preservation should eventually stop, given that industries other than steel are part of the Pittsburgh regional story and should also be remembered.

We intend that the activity of our Preservation Fund shall increase, since this supplies stop-gap financing that allows neighborhood preservation movements to secure historic properties until permanent financing is ready. We have found that the Fund is very successful as a leveraging element, and that demands upon it are growing.

Station Square will remain fundamental to Landmarks, a means by which it can increasingly approach self-support. Development will continue until the vacant land is improved and all 52 acres are a demonstration of the integration of historic preservation and modern development. At Station Square, the public will benefit from the ready access to the river and from a friendly, peaceful environment in which to shop, work, and eventually to live.

We see Station Square as an element of a chain of attractions toward whose completion we intend to work. The institutions that may gather and are gathering around the Point—Station Square, the Duquesne Incline, the Science Center, Three Rivers Stadium, Point State Park—may well be linked by various transportation means with attractions up the Monongahela River such as the new Sandcastle Beach of Kennywood Park and the industrial-history parks projected for Carrie Furnaces and the Pinkerton landing site. Such a chain of attractions would both thrill residents of the Pittsburgh region, mixing the revealed past and the enjoyable present, and attract visitors who would gain a sense of the region and its inhabitants in a variety of experiences.

This is as far as we can go at this point. We hope that, as unforeseen crises and opportunities arise, we will meet them imaginatively and with energy, seeking always what is best for the growth of Pittsburgh and its region.

A ''Lady of Stone'' arrives at the Old Post Office in 1973.

The Pittsburgh History &
Landmarks Foundation: 25 Years

1964

Beginning of 1964: James D. Van Trump and Arthur P. Ziegler, Jr., walking along Liverpool Street and apprehensive of urban renewal in Manchester, form the idea of a historic-preservation organization serving Allegheny County.

May, 1964: Van Trump and Ziegler, now on the staff of *Charette*, journal of the Pittsburgh Architectural Club, have organized the new group on an informal basis. Chatham Associates, publisher of *Charette*, offers use of its rooms at 503 Chamber of Commerce Building on Seventh Avenue. A study of the history, architecture, and population of the 1300 block of Liverpool Street, sponsored by Helen Clay Frick, is under way. The City Planning Department expresses appreciation of the need for such an organization to make surveys, offer advice, and advocate preservation, and the director Calvin Hamilton, along with *Charette*, acts as sponsor.

September 30, 1964: The Pittsburgh History & Landmarks Foundation begins existence as an independent non-profit corporation. To the media the new organization announces multiple goals: planning and preservation proposals, suggested legislation, purchase of buildings for restoration, publications, tours, lectures, and publicity. The first Board meeting is held in the afternoon, electing among others Charles C. Arensberg as president, Barbara D. Hoffstot and James D. Van Trump as vice-presidents, and Arthur P. Ziegler, Jr. as executive secretary. At this time one tour is scheduled, and the Liverpool Street study is still under way. A question on the Neville house in Collier Township raises the matter of whether activities should be limited to Pittsburgh alone. Ultimately, Landmarks' area of activity is established as Allegheny County.

Late 1964: Landmarks receives its first grant. Money from the Pittsburgh Foundation is spent to buy a slide projector for use in lectures furthering the cause of preservation.

1965

1965: "The Stones of Pittsburgh" publication series begins with *An Architectural Tour of Pittsburgh* by James D. Van Trump. Subsequent titles are *1300-1335 Liverpool Street, Manchester, Old Allegheny, Pittsburgh* (Van Trump, n.d.); *Legend in Modern Gothic: The Union Trust Building, Pittsburgh* (Van Trump, 1966); *Evergreen Hamlet* (Van Trump, n.d.); *Landmark Architecture of Allegheny County Pennsylvania* (Van Trump and Ziegler, 1967); *Pittsburgh's Neglected Gateway: The Rotunda of the Pennsylvania Railroad Station* (Van Trump, n.d.); *Birmingham, Pittsburgh's South Side* (Ziegler, 1968); *By Any Other Name: The Controversial Spelling of "Pittsburgh," or Why the "H"?* (Van Trump, n.d.); *A City's Living Memory* (Robert Cairns, n.d.); *The Gothic Revived*

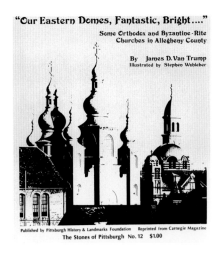

in Pittsburgh (Van Trump, 1975); *Station Square: A Golden Age Revived* (Van Trump, 1978); and *Our Eastern Domes, Fantastic, Bright...*(Van Trump, n.d.).

1965: Landmarks, too new to save the Allegheny Market House of 1863, records it and salvages decorative work.

1965: Landmarks begins its tour program. By 1989, this had expanded to include about 10 general membership tours and 30 privately-commissioned tours yearly, reaching approximately 1,600 people.

Early 1965: Landmarks moves to 404 Triangle Building at Seventh and Liberty Avenues.

1966

1966: The Sarah Scaife Foundation initiates Landmarks' Preservation Revolving Fund with a $100,000 grant and funds for administrative support. Monies from the Fund are used to purchase historic properties that Landmarks renovates and rents.

1966: Landmarks salvages interior and exterior decorative work from the Fourth Avenue Post Office in downtown Pittsburgh, under demolition. The work is complicated by official uncooperativeness, but public subscriptions and the good will of the demolition contractor make it possible to save the "Ladies of Stone," pediment sculptures by Eugenio Pedon. Finding a home for the sculptures is difficult, and in the course of time they change place several times. One group is now at Station Square, and one at the Allegheny Post Office (now the Pittsburgh Children's Museum) on the North Side.

March, 1966: The first issue of the Landmarks newsletter is published. A quarter-century later, *PHLF News* is an 11 1/2" x 17" eight-page quarterly newspaper, discussing Landmarks' preservation, education, Preservation Fund, and advocacy activities in detail, as well as discussing all notable preservation issues in and around Allegheny County.

Summer, 1966: Landmarks moves to 906 Benedum-Trees Building.

1967

1967: Landmarks begins bricks-and-mortar work in the Mexican War Streets area of the North Side. The objective is to preserve and rehabilitate the existing houses of this 19th-century residential area. A mixed-income, racially-integrated population is the goal, with minimum displacement of those already there.

1967: Landmarks encourages a "garden-block" program for the North Side, improving the appearance of residential blocks through planting, landscaping and painting as an encouragement to residents and lending institutions. The project is taken up by the Allegheny County Garden Club.

1967: Landmarks and Manchester citizens initiate and organize the United Manchester Redevelopment Corporation for the purposes of neighborhood revitalization and historic preservation. This is later renamed the Manchester Citizens Corporation. Landmarks and residents initiate the Manchester Program, the first program of the kind in the U.S. for low-income and minority families, to serve these purposes. Federal, State, City, and private money is used in the following years in programs whose purpose is to create a preserved, economically sound neighborhood affordable by the existing residents.

1967: Landmarks executes its first restoration in Manchester at 1329 Liverpool Street.

1967: Landmarks urges reproduction rather than removal of the finials on the towers of St. Mary's Church, Sharpsburg; this is done.

1967: A permanent loan of 4,000 volumes by James D. Van Trump forms the basis of Landmarks' James D. Van Trump Library, now in the Landmarks offices on the fourth floor of the Landmarks Building, Station Square.

Summer, 1967: *Landmark Architecture of Allegheny County, Pennsylvania* is published as the product of a two-year survey, conducted by Van Trump, Ziegler, and others. Besides listing many buildings virtually unknown thus far, the book recommends 12 historic-preservation districts.

1968

1968: Landmarks campaigns to save the "rotunda," the spectacular domed cab shelter of Union Station, the old Pennsylvania Railroad station at the entrance to the Strip district in downtown Pittsburgh. The building is to be demolished, making way for a business development to be called Penn Central Park. Local and national publications call attention to the campaign.

1968: Landmarks, with a grant from the Richard King Mellon Foundation, restores the Neill (or Neal) Log House in Schenley Park. The house of c. 1787, one of three surviving 18th-century buildings in Pittsburgh, has been neglected and in fact collapses while restoration plans are under way. Stotz, Hess & MacLachlan are the restoration architects.

Summer, 1968: Landmarks initiates the Birmingham Self-help Community Restoration Program. Co-sponsors are the South Side Chamber of Commerce and the South Side Community Council. The

program offers property owners free professional advice on facade restoration and on the raising of money for this purpose. Landmarks also devises a design scheme for planting, lighting, and sidewalk improvements on South Side streets that is accepted by the Pittsburgh Department of City Planning.

September 24, 1968: Landmarks' plaque program, with a grant from the Alcoa Foundation, begins with the installation of historic landmark plaques at the Allegheny County Courthouse, Allegheny County Jail, and Union Trust Building. By 1989, Landmarks has awarded over 200 plaques and made 93 successful nominations to the National Register of Historic Places.

1969

1969: Landmarks sponsors a competition of Carnegie-Mellon University architectural students to find a new use for the Union Station "rotunda," conceived as standing alone as an entrance feature of the proposed Penn Central Park.

1969: Landmarks begins its preservation services division for restoration and preservation advice, and also begins in-house design.

February, 1969: Landmarks initiates an experimental program in which it buys 1220 Monterey Street, restores it, and rents it back to the seller, the City's housing authority, for rental to low-income families. Under current Federal housing laws this is a promising means of providing restored low-cost housing, and this is the first employment of it in the U.S.

Spring, 1969: Landmarks receives a grant from the Federal and State highway administrations to photograph, make measured drawings of, and salvage fragments from North Side buildings condemned for the I-79 (later I-279) and adjacent road projects. The work continues through 1974 as buildings are cleared from Dutchtown northward.

Summer, 1969: Landmarks salvages decorative work from the Henry W. Oliver home on Ridge Avenue, about to be demolished with adjoining houses. Much of the material is re-used two years later in the Old Post Office Museum, in Allegheny Center.

1970

1970: Landmarks and community groups secure 7,000 petition signatures to begin restoration of the Allegheny Carnegie Library, promised by the City in 1968.

1970: Landmarks and the Carnegie Institute co-publish *An American Palace of Culture,* by James D. Van Trump.

1970: Landmarks hosts the Conference on Practical Preservation in Urban Areas, which gives national exposure to its work in inner-city areas.

1970: Working with local residents and the Pennsylvania Department of Highways, Landmarks devises a means of saving the Burtner house of 1821, in Harrison Township, from demolition in a road-building project. The Burtner House Society assumes ownership and restores the house for museum purposes.

1970: A grant from the Sarah Scaife Foundation forms the basis of a restoration revolving fund for the South Side.

1970: Landmarks acquires 1705 East Carson Street, an Italianate Building of c. 1870, to demonstrate economical but appropriate restoration.

Early 1970: The Urban Redevelopment Authority engages Landmarks to do a preservation study of Manchester, giving the comparative value of every building and making recommendations for the restoration of selected ones. Although Landmarks has done previous work for the URA, this is the first formal work.

Spring, 1970: The Mexican War Streets Society, a citizens' group for the improvement of the area, is founded at Landmarks' suggestion.

1971

1971: Landmarks campaigns for the re-erection of the Thomas A. Armstrong statue of 1889, damaged in 1969. In 1975 the restored statue is re-erected. Landmarks also campaigns to restore other public sculpture.

1971: Landmarks executes a historical study of the North Shore area of the North Side for the Urban Redevelopment Authority.

1971: Under the Historic American Engineering Record program, Landmarks records graphically and publishes a history of the Point and the Brady Street Bridges.

1971: Landmarks contracts with the County Commissioners to make recommendations for the revitalization of the Soldiers' and Sailors' Memorial.

1971: Landmarks encourages the priest and congregation of the Immaculate Heart of Mary Church, Polish Hill, in their successful efforts to save its prominent copper-clad domes. Further Landmarks' counseling in this matter becomes necessary in 1989.

Spring, 1971: A historic-preservation ordinance for the city of Pittsburgh, providing for a six-month delay in facade demolition or alteration of designated buildings, is enacted by City Council. Individual buildings and districts may be designated in this legislation, which Landmarks and the Department of City Planning had begun to draft in 1967.

Autumn, 1971: Landmarks moves from 906 Benedum-Trees Building to the old Allegheny Post Office on the North Side. The granite-faced Italian Renaissance building of 1897 had been intended by Pittsburgh's Urban Redevelopment Authority, in the mid-1960s, to go the way of almost everything else in central Allegheny and to be replaced by an apartment slab. *Landmark Architecture of Allegheny County* (1967), calls it "doomed." In the next year, though, Landmarks persuades the Urban Redevelopment Authority to spare the building and sell it to Landmarks for its offices and museum. Negotiations with the City and the State and solicitations of private funding secure the building. A design by Williams, Trebilcock and Whitehead inserts a new office mezzanine level. Decorative work from demolished Allegheny houses supplements the simple new construction. In January, 1972 the Old Post Office Museum is formally opened.

1972

1972: Landmarks protests the proposed demolition of the Byers-Lyon house on the North Side for a Community College of Allegheny County parking lot. In 1988 the house is generally restored for Community College use.

May, 1972: The National Trust for Historic Preservation gives Landmarks its citation for Significant Achievement in Historic Preservation.

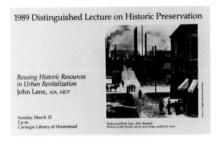

1989 Distinguished Lecture on Historic Preservation

Reusing Historic Resources in Urban Revitalization
John Lane, AIA, AICP

Sunday, March 12
2 p.m.
Carnegie Library of Homestead

September 25, 1972: Landmarks initiates its Distinguished Lecture Series with a talk by Leopold Adler II of the Historic Savannah Foundation. The lecture series continues generally on an annual basis. Leading figures in historic preservation are the speakers at the 21 lectures given through 1989.

1973

1973: In collaboration with the Hilltop Civic Improvement Association, Landmarks develops a program to revitalize the Allentown neighborhood of Pittsburgh.

1973: Landmarks develops plans, schematics, and economic projections for commercial and residential adaptation of the Colonial Trust Company, Peoples Bank, and Freehold Buildings in the Fourth Avenue financial area. Another developer adapts these buildings to different plans as the Bank Center.

Summer, 1973: The Walker-Ewing log house in Collier Township is donated to Landmarks. The house, said to be from the latter 18th century, is situated on a half-acre of land near Rennerdale. This is Landmarks' first historic-property gift.

December, 1973: Landmarks comments at length on the County's "Hall of Justice" proposal, anticipating replacement of the Courthouse in its traditional function. It suggests that Courthouse spaces can be used more intensively for purely court-related purposes, other County offices being put in the City-County Building. A further suggestion is that all City offices be moved to a restored and rehabilitated Union Station, which would be saved as the new City Hall (this does not happen). The bill funding the Hall of Justice is subsequently defeated.

1974

1974: Landmarks commissions a mural on a side wall of the L. M. Massey Shoe Company, 239 Fifth Avenue, as part of the building's exterior restoration. Landmarks is a consultant on the restoration as a part of a general downtown effort.

Spring, 1974: Landmarks undertakes an adaptive-use study of the Braddock Carnegie Library to determine its potential as a community-service building. Landmarks is asked to suggest possible uses rather than commenting on adaptability for a preconceived use.

Late 1974: Landmarks collaborates with the Borough of Springdale and the Landscape Design Society to form the Rachel Carson Homestead Association. The famous naturalist's home is to be used as a memorial and nature-study center.

1975

1975: James Van Trump discusses the history of Pittsburgh with Al Julius in brief segments on KDKA-TV, in a series that continues until 1978.

1975: Landmarks is commissioned by the Allegheny Conference on Community Development to do an architectural survey of all Golden Triangle buildings built before 1930. Of 480 buildings, 92 are regarded as of the highest quality.

1975: Landmarks studies residential and commercial adaptive use of the B&O Warehouse on the North Shore.

1975: Landmarks assists the borough of Glenfield with problems caused by the I-79 property taking.

1975: Landmarks publishes *Allegheny*, a history and present-day view of the North Side, by Walter C. Kidney and Arthur P. Ziegler, Jr.

1975: Landmarks publishes *The Walker-Ewing Log House*, by James D. Van Trump.

1975: Landmarks acquires the Victorian Gothic Henderson-Metz house in Fineview to hold for restoration. Restoration is completed by a purchaser in 1984, the interior being converted into seven apartments.

Late 1975: Landmarks and an auxiliary volunteer committee begin a drive to raise $250,000 to restore the Phipps Conservatory. The Committee for the Restoration of Phipps Conservatory finds extensive trouble with the physical plant, and in collaboration with the

City and with the use of public and private funds, makes the most pressing restorations. In 1985 a new independent group, Phipps Friends, assumes restoration and maintenance responsibilities.

1976

1976: Landmarks executes an architectural survey of Oakland.

1976: Landmarks acquires "Woodville," the Presley Neville house of c. 1785 and after in Collier Township. The Neville House Auxiliary is formed in 1978 to raise funds and begin the work of restoration that still continues.

1976: Landmarks collaborates with the County Parks Department to convert the courtyard of the Courthouse, long a parking lot, into a park. Landmarks and County employees supply the design; Landmarks obtains $64,000 from the Sarah Scaife Foundation for materials; the County supplies labor.

1976: Landmarks is active in a variety of bicentennial projects including a festival at Point Park and publishes a brochure describing historical and cultural attractions in Allegheny County.

June 15, 1976: Landmarks announces the Station Square project, a mixture of restored existing buildings and new construction on the 42-acre Pittsburgh & Lake Erie Railroad terminal property across the Monongahela River from Pittsburgh. A $5 million grant from the Allegheny Foundation begins the work.

November 1, 1976: Landmarks holds the "I Spy Pittsburgh" seminar and walking tour on local history as a Bicentennial event. *Pittsburgh Treasure Hunt*, the first Landmarks publication for children and written by Patricia Wiley, is used as a text and is published separately; this is reissued in 1981.

1977

1977: Landmarks and the Junior League of Pittsburgh collaborate to acquire 841 Lincoln Avenue in Allegheny West for preservation.

1977: The National Endowment for the Arts, under its City Scale program, awards Landmarks a grant to study redesign of Allegheny Square, North Side; Doughboy Square, Lawrenceville; Oakland Square, South Oakland; the Schenley Fountain area, Schenley Park; Magee Square, Triangle; and the open areas of Station Square.

1977: The Express House, the first rehabilitated building of Station Square, is reopened. It has three floors, with about 10,000 square feet.

1977: Landmarks publishes *The Olden Triangle*, by Urban Design Associates, as a part of its continuing downtown restoration program.

1977: Landmarks studies Union Station for the Federal Railways Administration. The original mandate specifies studying feasibility of conversion into an intermodal transportation and cultural center. Landmarks' conclusion is that such conversion is not practical, but that re-use as a 300-room hotel serving the nearby Convention Center is feasible. The City rejects Landmarks' offer to undertake the development, preferring a new hotel building.

1977: Landmarks and a local group form the Old St. Luke's Auxiliary to look after the rehabilitation of St. Luke's Episcopal Church, a Gothic church of 1852 in Woodville, Collier Township. By 1989 the church is very nearly restored, with some site improvements still to be executed.

1977: Landmarks hosts its first annual Antiques Show, a fall event that becomes the most successful fundraiser each year, and the most prestigious antiques show in the area. By 1989, 30 dealers attend, and several thousand people.

1978

1978: Landmarks studies the Pittsburgh & Lake Erie Railroad station at Coraopolis for its potential as a restaurant, and concludes that the re-use is feasible.

April 28, 1978: The 550-seat Grand Concourse restaurant, the first at Station Square, is opened. The interiors of the old passenger waiting rooms, luggage room, and covered outside walk are restored and adapted to the purpose.

Summer, 1978: The Three Rivers Regatta, a weekend celebration of recreation on and beside the rivers, is held for the first time. Landmarks is a co-sponsor through 1987.

1979

1979: With the Allegheny Conference and Pittsburgh's City Planning Department, Landmarks sponsors the Conference on the Re-use of Downtown Buildings. Re-use of specific Triangle buildings, considering design and economics, is discussed before 200 attending.

1979: Landmarks salvages woodwork and glass from the Phipps-Braun house, on Warwick Terrace in Squirrel Hill. St. Brendan's Crossing and others in the Shops at Station Square use some of the decorative work.

1979: Landmarks begins the Allegheny County section of the Pennsylvania Historic Resource Survey, in which 6,114 buildings, structures, and places from before 1940 will be recorded over a four-year period.

1979: Landmarks serves as consultant to the City on restoration of the South Side Market House, which it had long been advocating.

January, 1979: Mann's Hotel, a wooden tavern built in McKees Rocks at various periods in the 19th century, is saved from demolition for a bridge reconstruction. Landmarks had participated with others in a three-year struggle to have the bridge itself and its approaches redesigned so as not to require taking of the hotel.

Spring, 1979: Bessemer Court, the main pedestrian exterior space of Station Square, begins to take form as the 1930 Bessemer converter, from the Ambridge plant of the A. M. Byers Company, is erected. Although the Bessemer process is best known as the first producer of high-volume steel, this converter made wrought iron by the Aston-Byers process. Donors are Gerald Peckich and Arthur Silverman, with financial help by the Engineers Society of Western Pennsylvania for the erection.

September, 1979: The Freight House Shops, the first retail area at Station Square, is opened. The four-aisled, 45-shop building had originally been a transfer facility, built in 1897, between freight cars and wagons.

1980

1980: Landmarks publishes *Street Cars in Literature*, edited by Harold M. Englund.

1980: Landmarks does a complete architectural survey of Tarentum.

April, 1980: The Langenheim house of 1883 at 1315 Liverpool Street, Manchester, rescued from demolition at the request of neighbors, is opened as an eight-unit apartment house, completing a 12-year restoration and remodeling campaign.

June, 1980: Landmarks completes a preservation and restoration study of 14 buildings belonging to Allegheny Cemetery. Restoration, administered by the Allegheny Cemetery Historical Association, begins shortly after.

1981

1981: Landmarks restores two workers' houses, built c. 1850 by the Penn Salt Company in Natrona, for sale.

1981: Landmarks publishes *Famous Men and Women of Pittsburgh*, edited by Leonore Elkus and based on a lecture series sponsored by Landmarks and given during the U.S. Bicentennial.

1982

1982: Landmarks and the Gifted and Talented Education Program of the Allegheny Intermediate Unit initiate the "An Eye for Architecture" slide/tape program for elementary and secondary school grades with funding support from the National Endowment for the Arts. Subject areas of the programs are toured after the presentation.

1982: Landmarks publishes *The Three Rivers*, a book about the past and present significance of the Ohio, Monongahela, and Allegheny Rivers by Walter C. Kidney.

1982: Landmarks begins a series of commercial and oral histories with *John M. Roberts and Son Company, 1832-1982*. Later titles are *The Papercraft Story* by Frances C. Hardie, and *Sarah,* by Sarah Evosevich *et al.*

1982: Landmarks initiates its Award of Merit program for persons and organizations that have furthered the causes of historic preservation and historical knowledge in Allegheny County. As of 1989, about 70 projects had been recognized.

1982: The Shovel Transfer Warehouse of 1917 at Station Square reopens as Commerce Court, with 15 retail businesses and 334,000 square feet of office space on six upper floors. An 800-car parking garage, a new construction, opens to its immediate west.

1982: Landmarks begins its first major capital-fund campaign, with a goal of $2.3 million. The campaign is intended to support Landmarks' work in five major areas: historic buildings development; museums and special projects; the revolving/endangered buildings fund; public education; and endowment. The fund-raising goal is reached in 1985. More than 300 foundations, businesses, and individuals contribute, reflecting a broad base of community support and providing Landmarks with a firm operating base.

1982: Landmarks initiates its slide-show lending library. By 1989, this has 12 slide shows featuring Pittsburgh's history, architecture, ethnic character, parks, and public sculpture. Many schools and community groups are borrowers.

1982: Landmarks proposes that the new Pittsburgh Children's Museum occupy the Old Post Office.

1983

1983: Landmarks proposes that, when the Jenkins Arcade building is demolished, arcade space be created in the replacement building, Fifth Avenue Place; this is done.

1983: Landmarks opposes demolition of the facade of the Loyal Order of Moose Building, 626 Penn Avenue. Demolition is found to be inevitable after a cooperative study by Landmarks, the City, and the Heinz interests active in the area. Landmarks works with State and City agencies to create a new Penn-Liberty Historic District, between Seventh and Tenth Streets, whose buildings will be documented and restored.

1983: At Station Square, the old P&LE passenger station (housing the Grand Concourse since 1978) is reopened in full as the Landmarks Building. At the same time the Annex, at the corner of Smithfield and Carson Streets, is reopened as the Gatehouse.

1983: Landmarks holds the "Gallery Lectures," an informal lunch-time slide-lecture series, at the Old Post Office Museum. The lectures are repeated in 1984.

PITTSBURGH HERITAGE

An Exploration of Pittsburgh History & Architecture through Workshop Activities, Walking Tours and Field Trips

1983: Landmarks initiates "Pittsburgh Heritage," an eight-day summer workshop for elementary and secondary students and teachers, with funding support from the Henry C. Frick Educational Commission. A session is held annually.

1983: Landmarks initiates its Architectural Apprenticeship Program, sponsored by the Gifted and Talented Program of the Allegheny Intermediate Unit, for high school students. Tours, lectures, slide shows, and building visits are scheduled during the five-session course. The program is offered each succeeding year.

Spring, 1983: The Pittsburgh Children's Museum moves into the Old Post Office.

November 11, 1983: Landmarks publishes *Life and Architecture in Pittsburgh*, a collection of the essays and radio talks of James D. Van Trump. Originally hardbound, it is later issued in paperback.

1984

December 20, 1984: Landmarks announces a Claude Worthington Benedum Foundation grant award of $200,000 to create Landmarks' Revolving Fund for Education. Revenue from fees for educational work will help replenish the fund, which will also strengthen existing programs in tours, lectures, exhibits, publications, and student/teacher workshops.

1985

1985: Landmarks moves to Suite 450, The Landmarks Building, Station Square. The Old Post Office on the North Side is now wholly occupied by the Pittsburgh Children's Museum.

1985: Landmarks performs two thematic nominations to the National Register of Historic Places: one of seven Allegheny County river bridges, one of 49 Pittsburgh public schools.

1985: The Station Square Transportation Museum, a project led by a Landmarks' trustee, G. Whitney Snyder, opens in an old boiler house in Bessemer Court. Plans for a greatly-expanded museum are proposed in 1988.

1985: Landmarks creates a slide show and tour manual on the Neill Log House in Schenley Park; in collaboration with the Junior League of Pittsburgh, it offers summer weekend tours of the house.

1985: Landmarks creates and offers two teacher in-service courses, "Exploring Your Neighborhood Through History and Architecture" and "Exploring Your City: Pittsburgh's Past and Present." These are offered regularly through the Allegheny Intermediate Unit.

1985: Landmarks creates the traveling exhibits *Landmark Survivors* and *Architecture: The Building Art* with funding support from the Henry C. Frick Educational Commission and PPG Industries Foundation, respectively. Each year, on an average, an exhibit travels to six schools and community groups. Each exhibit has a printed guide.

1985: Having completed a National Register nomination for Schenley Park, Landmarks asks the Western Pennsylvania Conservancy to co-sponsor the Schenley Park Restoration Project, which is to include planning, research, fundraising, promotion, and restoration, and is intended to be well advanced by the time of the Park centennial in 1989.

1985: Landmarks initiates its Preservation Fund, a loan fund created by the sale of properties that had been restored in the 1960s and '70s by Landmarks' Revolving Fund first established in 1966. The new money is available to non-profit neighborhood organizations and individuals to serve as stop-gap or bridge financing for restoration projects. The first loans are to the Rachel Carson Homestead Association ($5,700 for architectural services); the Mexican War Streets Society ($31,500 for facade lighting); Hollander Associates ($100,000 to buy the Hollander Building in Dutchtown); and the Ben Avon Area Historical Association ($10,000 for the site preparation and construction for the Dickson Log House in Ben Avon).

As a part of its Preservation Fund activity, Landmarks offers technical assistance to the following organizations: Allegheny West Civic Council; Bureau of Historic Preservation, Commonwealth of Pennsylvania; Calbride Place Citizens Council; Central Northside Neighborhood Council; Coalition for Low-Income Housing; East Allegheny Community Council; Hill District Development Corporation; Manchester Citizens Corporation; Mexican War Streets Society; Neighborhood Centers Association; Northside Civic Development Council; Northside Tenants Reorganization; Peoples Oakland Planning and Development Corporation;

Pittsburgh Board of Code Review; Pittsburgh Community Services and Block Grant Program; Pittsburgh Community Technical Assistance Center; Pittsburgh Neighborhood Fund; Preservation Action; Southside Local Development Corporation; United Way of Allegheny County; and University of Pittsburgh Community Internship Programs. The number of these organizations continues to increase.

1985: Landmarks becomes managing partner in a joint ownership of the Lawrence Paint Building, just beyond the original western end of Station Square. It suggests the building for the home of the new History Center proposed for Pittsburgh at a meeting of historical organizations that it convokes on March 5. The History Center project is later assumed by the Historical Society of Western Pennsylvania.

Summer, 1985. Landmarks and the Neville House Auxiliary host the first annual antiques show at the Neville House in Collier Township. The show is set outdoors on the landscaped grounds of the house.

July 27, 1985: Landmarks holds a public forum for discussion of preservation and development in the Strip district.

September, 1985: Landmarks publishes *Landmark Architecture: Pittsburgh and Allegheny County*. This is based on the Allegheny County part of the Pennsylvania Historic Resource Survey, completed by Landmarks in 1984, and replaces *Landmark Architecture of Allegheny County* (1967), long out of print. Walter C. Kidney is the principal author.

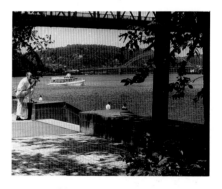

Winter, 1985/86: Landmarks publishes two planning statements in *PHLF News.* One concerns the Strip and urges that its present function as a low-rent food wholesale and retail center be continued, while a "festive" retail center proposed for the Strip be abandoned. The other statement envisions an expanding tourist industry based on coordinated and connected features on all rivers adjacent to the Point, using aerial tramways and river boats. These attractions would be the subject of a national marketing program, to which, after 1988, Landmarks will devote its attention.

1986

1986: Landmarks' "Hands-On History," a summer institute for teachers funded by the Pennsylvania Humanities Council, is first offered in a five-day session for 75 elementary and secondary-school teachers. By 1989 the institute will have been offered four times.

1986: Landmarks initiates the Home Ownership for Working People project, which with the collaboration of several public and private agencies makes ownership of restored houses possible to low-income families.

St. Mary's

E & O Brewery

1986: The Preservation Fund makes loans for five projects: Home Ownership for Working People ($100,000 to acquire and restore five Central North Side houses); St. Mary's Priory ($50,000 for acquisition); Eberhardt & Ober Brewery ($50,000 for acquisition); New Bethel Church, Lawrenceville ($7,400 for roof repairs); and the Braddock Carnegie Library ($2,500 for a re-use study).

December 6, 1986: The first "Hands-On History Festival" is sponsored by Landmarks. This event is repeated on March 26, 1988 and April 15, 1989, with growing attendance. The purpose is to show the work of Landmarks' education department. Hundreds of teachers and pupils display projects on Pittsburgh historical and architectural themes, and enter hand-made bridges in the "Great Pittsburgh Bridge-building Contest."

1987

1987: Landmarks completes a survey of 80 known extant works of the Pittsburgh architect Frederick G. Scheibler, Jr. for the Pennsylvania Historical and Museum Commission. Of these, 32 are found National Register-eligible in addition to two already on the Register.

1987: Landmarks completes a survey of historic resources in the iron and steel industry in Allegheny and three adjacent counties. The survey, made for the Pennsylvania Historical and Museum Commission, identifies remains of 32 plants extant before 1945 and finds six of them National Register-eligible.

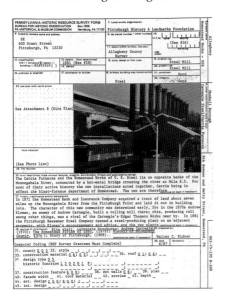

1987: Landmarks supplies information for an Environmental Impact Statement for several possible routes of the Mon Valley Expressway within Allegheny County.

1987: Landmarks publishes *Sarah: Her Life, Her Restaurant, Her Recipes*. This is the life of Sarah Vukelich Evosevich, Serbian immigrant and South Side restaurant proprietress, told largely in her own words.

1987: Landmarks creates and offers the teacher in-service course "Exploring Architecture" for elementary and secondary teachers. The course is offered regularly through the Allegheny Intermediate Unit.

1987: Landmarks, a land lessee of the Pittsburgh & Lake Erie Railroad since 1976, buys the land of Station Square. It owns 52 acres by 1989, including the separately-purchased Lawrence Paint property.

1987: Landmarks and the Allegheny County Commissioners establish the Courthouse Restoration Committee.

1987: The Preservation Fund lends money for the following projects: Anderson Manor ($100,000 for restoration); Western Avenue Associates ($80,000 to acquire and restore 901-05 Western Avenue, Allegheny West); 1417 East Carson Street ($39,500 for acquisition and restoration).

Fall, 1987: The Regional Industrial Development Corporation requests Landmarks to survey the National and Duquesne Works of USX for artifact, archival, and structural preservation.

1988

1988: Landmarks' Preservation Fund staff assembles 18 neighborhood organizations into the Pittsburgh Community Reinvestment Group, which obtains a pledge of $109 million from Union National Bank for community reinvestment purposes.

1988: The Preservation Fund lends money for the following projects: Allequippa Place ($150,000 for restoration); Masonic Temple, Central North Side ($100,000 for acquisition); Brighton Place Housing Co-operatives, Manchester ($45,000 for acquisition); Mechanic's Retreat, Mexican War Streets ($2,500 gift for park maintenance).

1988: Landmarks receives a matching grant from the National Trust to develop a preservation handbook for the Courthouse and Jail.

1988: Landmarks publishes *Pittsburgh in Your Pocket*, a small guide to 64 local landmarks by Walter C. Kidney, with partial funding assistance from the Historical Foundation of Pennsylvania.

February 18, 1988: Landmarks hosts a conference on preservation of steel-plant structures, and in cooperation with the National Park Service helps organize the multi-organizational Steel Industry Heritage Task Force, whose first meeting is May 16. Landmarks provides staff and funding for the first two years. The purpose of the Steel Industry Heritage Task Force is to preserve sites and artifacts of historic value associated with the steel industry of the Pittsburgh region. The draft Action Plan of the Task Force is published November 30.

September 24, 1988: On the occasion of the Allegheny County Bicentennial and the centennial of the dedication of the County Buildings, Landmarks releases *Majesty of the Law: The Court Houses of Allegheny County*, by James D. Van Trump.

November 1, 1988: Landmarks initiates the "Portable Pittsburgh" docent-outreach program, centered around a trunk packed with typical historic artifacts that illustrate the Pittsburgh past. The program was created through a grant from the Henry C. Frick Educational Commission. More than 150 sessions of "Portable Pittsburgh" are offered to schools by Landmarks' volunteers in the first five months of the program.

December 15, 1988: Landmarks announces its Riverside Industrial Walk, a mile promenade at Station Square displaying massive industrial artifacts. The first object dedicated is a 20-ton ingot mold from Shenango, Inc.

1989

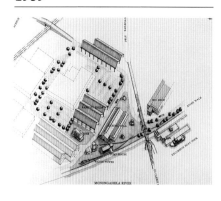

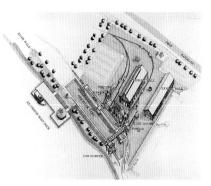

1989: As a member of the Steel Industry Heritage Task Force, Landmarks helps secure $350,000 in federal funds to support formal studies of selected historic steel sites in Allegheny County, and in March submits a 1990 federal budget request for continuing support. The Task Force contracts Landmarks Design As-

sociates to develop preliminary conceptual designs for the development of the Carrie Furnaces Nos. 6 and 7 in Swissvale and the Pinkerton landing site at the Homestead Works in Munhall as museum sites, and engages consultants to carry out marketing and financial feasibility studies. The Historic American Engineering Record office of the National Park Service conducts documentation projects of seven steel sites. These and other studies are to be completed by October 1, when the Task Force will initiate a private-sector fund-raising drive to support the purchase of 30 to 40 acres at the Homestead Works and Carrie Furnaces sites.

852 Beech Street

1989: The Preservation Fund assists the following: Manchester Citizens Corporation (loans of $45,000 for 852 Beech Street, $145,000 for five Manchester houses, $47,231 for 1256-58 Decatur Street, $50,687 for 1131 N. Franklin Street, and $47,080 for 1109 Manhattan Street, $1.00 for 1418 Columbus Avenue, as well as technical assistance for the 1300 block of Sheffield Street); and Northside Tenants Reorganization ($45,000 for Brighton Place).

1989: Landmarks assists the Carnegie Library of Homestead in raising money for operating and restoration costs.

1989: Landmarks opposes a threat to St. Peter's Episcopal Church in Oakland, and works with the Diocese, parishioners, Oaklanders, and the City Planning Department to find a means of saving it.

April, 1989: Through a matching grant from the Pennsylvania Historical and Museum Commission, Landmarks conducts a National Register District Survey of the Homestead area.

May 17, 1989: Through the Preservation Fund, Landmarks co-sponsors a lecture presented by Ms. Bertha Gilkey, president of the Cochran Tenant Management Corporation in St. Louis. Ms. Gilkey speaks to neighborhood groups on tenant management of low-income housing.

June, 1989: Thanks to the Neville House Advisory Committee, the Colonial Dames, and the Neville House Auxiliary, the Neville house in Collier Township opens on weekends in June for public house tours for the first time in its 200-year history. The living room, dining room, and hall are restored to their original 18th-century condition and furnished according to General John Neville's original inventory of 1790.

July, 1989: Landmarks offers a special church tour and announces that it plans to publish a book featuring more than 45 Pittsburgh-area churches. The tour and publication are created by Landmarks in conjunction with a WQED-TV documentary titled *Holy Pittsburgh* that is first broadcast on June 21.

July, 1989: Landmarks secures two major grants to augment the working assets of its Revolving Fund for Education.

August, 1989: A colorful membership brochure is printed for Landmarks, and a membership challenge is announced in the fall issue of *PHLF News*.

September 24, 1989: At the end of its twenty-fifth year, the Pittsburgh History & Landmarks Foundation, which began with two part-time salaried staff, now has 73 trustees, an office staff of 13, and a grounds crew of 11, as well as 25 docents and 85 other volunteers. Landmarks publishes a quarterly eight-page newsletter, and, in general, one book a year. It offers about 10 public and 30 private tours annually, and reaches the public as well through its "Hands-On History Festival" and its educational workshops and traveling exhibits. As an advisor and board member it participates in the activities of over 20 neighborhood, municipal, state, and national organizations. Its Preservation Fund has lent $1,037,000, as of mid-1989, for restorations and historic-housing rehabilitation, the latter for low- and moderate-income residents. Landmarks has hosted and has participated in conferences on preservation and related matters since its earliest years.

Station Square, Landmarks' 52-acre development on the Pittsburgh & Lake Erie Station site, is a combination of luxury retail shops and restaurants, offices, and historic displays in six buildings. The total investment in Station Square has been $80,000,000, and the development pays over $2,500,000 a year in taxes, and attracts more than three million people. It not only generates income for Landmarks that is invested in further development, but illustrates the return to usefulness of an underused historic area, attracts visitors to Pittsburgh, and gives life to the city on evenings and weekends.

On this day, September 24, there is a 25-year commemorative tour of neighborhoods where Landmarks has made a difference. Afterward, there is a champagne reception, and Arthur P. Ziegler, Jr. presents the first copy of this book to Charles C. Arensberg, chairman of Landmarks' board, to whom it is dedicated.

Index

A Past Still Alive was typeset in Paladium by Cold Comp and was printed on 80lb. Vintage Velvet text by Herrmann Printing & Litho, Inc. The publication was designed by Thomas S. Stevenson, Jr. of Landmarks Design Associates, with assistance from Jean Hodak.